DOWN
AMONGST
THE BLACK
GANG

DOWN AMONGST THE BLACK GANG

THE WORLD AND WORKPLACE OF RMS *TITANIC*'S STOKERS

RICHARD P. DE KERBRECH

The History Press

For Hilary

Frontispiece: Canadian Pacific's *Empress of Britain* of 1906, with boilers being tended. Note to left, the large pieces of coal which need to be broken down into smaller pieces to fit a shovel, and to the right the watertight door to the firemen's passage. (Author's collection)

First published 2014

The History Press
The Mill, Brimscombe Port
Stroud, Gloucestershire, GL5 2QG
www.thehistorypress.co.uk

© Richard P. de Kerbrech 2014

The right of Richard P. de Kerbrech to be identified as the Author
of this work has been asserted in accordance with the
Copyright, Designs and Patents Act 1988.

British Library Cataloguing in Publication Data.
A catalogue record for this book is available from the British Library.

ISBN 978 0 7524 9323 7

Typesetting and origination by The History Press
Printed in Great Britain

CONTENTS

ACKNOWLEDGEMENTS

I should like to extend my gratitude and acknowledgement to the following persons, firms and institutions for their kindness in contributing information and illustrations and other help, and without whose assistance this book would certainly not have been written.

Of necessity, a project of this nature draws heavily on a vast wealth of previously published sources. Chief among these, being *The Marine Steam Engine* by R. Sennett and H.J. Oram, and *Engine Room Practice* by John G. Liversidge, both of which were published in Edwardian times. More recently, the *Haynes RMS Titanic Owners' Workshop Manual* has proved to be a valuable source of reference. Of the illustrations, the images of the *Olympic*, *Titanic* and *Britannic*'s boilers, main engines, turbines and auxiliaries and parts under construction have been gleaned from a number of sources and credited as such. However, they were all originally created by the professional photographer Robert John Welch (1859–1936) and on some images his initials may be seen. From 1894 up until the First World War he worked as Harland & Wolff's official photographer.

My thanks go initially to Nigel Overton, City and Maritime Heritage Curator at Plymouth City Museum and Art Gallery, for germinating the idea for this work.

To the following for their support and sharing their technical knowledge: to my old friend David Hutchings, an authority on the *Titanic*, for his technical advice and uses of images from his collection, Samuel Halpern, Simon Mills, John Siggins, Alan McCartney of the Ulster Folk & Transport Museum and Michelle Ambrose of the National Museums Northern Ireland, Maurizio Eliseo, Encyclopedia-Titanica, the Imperial War Museum, the Public Record Office of Northern Ireland, the United

States Naval Historical Centre, Brian Ticehurst, Claes-Göran Wetterholm and Richard Woodman. Finally, to David Williams my good friend, former professional photographer and co-author on previous books, who with his usual enthusiasm gave his time and advice on picture selection and image quality.

Members of the Black Gang of Lloyd Sabaudo's 1907-built *Tomaso di Savoia* who worked in the boiler rooms and bunker spaces, blackened by the coal dust and grime. These men were rarely encountered by passengers. In this group, during 1927, all are wearing head gear, and the two engineers are rigged in boiler suits and peaked caps. (Maurizio Eliseo collection)

INTRODUCTION

Much has been written and documented about the *Titanic* disaster, but this work seeks to concentrate on the actual world and workplace of the *Titanic's* Black Gang. In doing so there will be an opportunity to take a journey and have a detailed look at some of the major elements of machinery that one might also have encountered in the engine and boiler rooms of the RMS *Titanic* and her sister ships, the *Olympic* and *Britannic*. This work does not deal with the engine room personnel as individual cases but rather from the human and social factor, with generic descriptions of their jobs and life in the stokehold. This to some may seem somewhat stereotypical. It also deals in some small part with the heroic efforts of the engine room personnel who tried in vain to save the ship following its collision with the iceberg.

As strange as it may seem, no known photographs of the engine and boiler rooms, with machinery in place, of the *Olympic*, *Titanic* and *Britannic* (Yard Nos 400, 401 and 433) exist. None even of firemen/stokers at work in their boiler rooms and stokeholds. This seems somewhat ironical when one considers that the *Olympic* was not converted to oil-burning until 1919–20!

In an attempt to help compensate for this, any images are from coal-burning vessels contemporaneous with the 'Olympic'-class ships, such as French Line's *France* of 1912 and Cunard's *Aquitania* of 1914. The United States Naval Historical Centre have preserved boiler room images of the US Navy's troopships *George Washington*, *Leviathan*, *Mount Vernon* and *Troy*. All were built during the Edwardian era and just before the First World War. Three were commandeered German liners: the *George Washington* completed in 1908 was formerly owned by North German Lloyd; the

Mount Vernon had been the same company's *Kronprinzessen Cecilie* completed in 1906; and the *Leviathan* had been Hamburg America Line's *Vaterland*, completed in 1914. They were more than likely manned by US Navy conscripts (US: 'draftees'). Other scenes are from merchant vessels of the coal-burning era, and with one exception show the stokeholds with fire tube, cylindrical or 'Scotch' boilers. Most of these engine room photographs may have been posed for the time exposure of film used in its day. Hopefully they may help show the harsh conditions of extreme heat, dimly lit, dirty, and back-breaking environment in which the Black Gang toiled. Indeed some are even somewhat 'Gothic' in appearance. Originally the Black Gang, also known as the 'Black Feet Brigade', were the firemen/ stokers and trimmers who worked in the stokeholds and boiler rooms of coal-burning steamships like the *Titanic*. Their name derived from their black appearance due to the coating of coal dust on their faces, exposed skin and clothing, and the hot, coal-dust laden atmosphere in which they laboured. Along with coal miners, foundry workers and chimney sweeps, it was a dirty, filthy, grimy job, but unlike these two trades, firemen and trimmers also had to endure the searing heat from open furnaces. In time this would apply to anyone who worked down below among the Black Gang, like greasers, and also the engineers could be labelled by the same familiar (or perhaps derogatory) sobriquet.

The title of fireman or stoker is interchangeable, as in time the actual distinction has become blurred. It is believed that the title stoker was a Royal Navy rating, while fireman applied to the same post in the Merchant Navy and essentially their work was the same. It has been written in Commander (E) A. Funge Smith's book *Introduction to Marine Engineering* that 'there are no stokers in the Merchant Navy, the nearest approach to them being the firemen who attend to the fires of the boiler furnaces ...'

The *Titanic* had twenty-four double-ended boilers and five single-ended boilers. When all the double-enders were fully fired up and operational, they could consume approximately 850 tons of coal per day, or on average 35 tons per hour, and the *Titanic* had a total bunker capacity of 6,611 tons. It was the Black Gang's job to keep these boilers fed, which meant shovelling a ton of coal into the boiler furnaces every two minutes. Every boiler room was manned by ten firemen and four trimmers. Rarely seen or encountered by the passengers, the Black Gang provided the manpower behind the horsepower.

The stokehold and boiler rooms as terms were also interchangeable, but on the *Titanic* the boiler rooms were separated by watertight bulkheads, and the stokeholds were the transverse 'alleys' from the amidships line of the hull where the boiler fronts were worked.

Where possible descriptions of the *Titanic*'s boilers and main engines are from the ship's actual technical specifications. When these have not been available, technical details from Marine Engineering and Naval Architecture literature contemporaneous with the era of the *Titanic* are used. As the *Titanic* was the second of a class of three ships, her earlier sister, the *Olympic*, has been referred to, as has the last of the trio, the *Britannic*. Also illustrations and descriptions from those of her sister ships have been used.

In a work of this nature which has a large amount of technical content it has be necessary to use a degree of technical terms and expressions. Regrettably this has been unavoidable and apologies are due to the general readership who may be from a non-technical background. In order to make the content a little more digestible, where possible the chapters have been arranged in an alternate technical description and social history/ human element fashion. All units are in imperial quantities as befitting those used in shipyards of the day, the exception being electrical power which is quoted in watts (W) or kilowatts (kW).

Where displacement tonnages have been referred to, and masses and weights of machinery and bunker coal, imperial tons have been used (made up of 2,240lb) which are referred to in the United States as 'long tons'.

During the Edwardian era and indeed up until 1922, the Merchant Navy was known as the Mercantile Marine, Merchant Service or Merchant Marine. The British Board of Trade (BoT) was the government department chiefly concerned with safety at sea, the survey of ships in its hands and the examination of Mercantile Marine officers for their Certificates of Competency ('tickets').

Harland & Wolff's 'Olympic'-class Passenger Vessels

The White Star Line, which began trading as a transatlantic steamship company in 1869, declared a policy of placing supreme comfort and size before speed, with the introduction of the innovative *Oceanic* of 1899. This move gained the company a considerable following with the travelling public, and a reputation for excellence. In 1902 the company was taken over by John Pierpont Morgan's large United States shipping combine, the International Mercantile Marine Company (IMMCo) but still traded as the White Star Line.

By 1908 an emigrant could travel to the United States for just £2 ($10) and J.P. Morgan foresaw fixed prices in the hope of eliminating competition. However, for J. Bruce Ismay, then the chairman of White Star, one of the answers to the stiff competition from Cunard and other shipping companies from the continent, was to build larger and finer ships with greater carrying capacity. It was decided to build a class of three large vessels of immense size, which would later become the *Olympic, Titanic* and *Britannic* (originally proposed as the *Gigantic*).

The Harland & Wolff team responsible for the design of the 'Olympic'-class comprised Lord Pirrie, Thomas Andrews, the managing director of the design department, Lord Pirrie's nephew; Edward Wilding, deputy to Andrews and responsible for the design calculations, stability and trim; and finally Alexander M. Carlisle, Harland & Wolff's Chief Naval Architect.

Although the *Olympic* was the first of the class to be laid down and built, the *Titanic's* life began with the laying of her keel on 31 March 1909 as Yard No 401. At the time of the construction of the *Olympic* and *Titanic*, Harland & Wolff had a workforce of around 14,000 men, and at any time between 3,000 and 4,000 of these would be allocated to the building of the two sisters.

Her construction was of the traditional keel, 300 frames, rib and beam type rising upwards from the keel like a skeleton of some huge steel dinosaur. Shop managers, foremen, craftsmen, labourers and apprentices referred to detailed drawings, and from these manufactured from steel, wood, copper, brass and glass the frames, plates, engines, boilers and thousands of other items that would together create the largest ship ever built to that date.

The *Titanic* like the *Olympic* was constructed of mild steel with cellular double bottoms 5ft 3in deep. The bottom plating was hydraulically riveted; the strakes were arranged in clincher fashion and the underside of the framing was joggled to avoid the use of tapered packing pieces. In order to reduce the number of butts and overlaps to a minimum, plates of a large size for their day were adopted, some 2,000 in all. The shell plates were from 30ft to 36ft long and 6ft wide; the largest plates weighed some 4½ tons. Steel plates used in the construction of her keel and the adjacent strakes were 1in thick, as were plates used at the waterline and the turn of bilge; however, plates used at the sheer strake were doubled for extra strength in this region. In all some 2 million rivets were used in her overall construction.

The hull was subdivided by fifteen transverse watertight bulkheads which created sixteen compartments. The watertight doors to these were electrically controlled from the bridge and should any two of the largest compartments become flooded, the vessel could remain afloat indefinitely. These safeguards led White Star to believe that the ship was practically unsinkable. As stated, in the event of an emergency, the *Titanic* had been designed to remain afloat with any two of her watertight compartments fully flooded. However, on the night of her collision with an iceberg the starboard hull along the first five compartments was breached and laid open to the sea. Her watertight integrity was compromised and the ship's fate sealed.

There were eight steel decks amidships: A, the boat or promenade deck; B, the bridge deck; C, the shelter deck; D, the saloon deck; E, the upper deck; F, the middle deck; and G, the lower deck. At the ends an orlop deck was fitted, which made nine decks in all.

Accommodation was provided for 739 first-class, 674 second-class and 1,026 third-class passengers. In addition the *Titanic* had a crew of about 899 and was capable of carrying some 3,300 persons in total.

The *Titanic*'s huge structure rose in the gantry against the Belfast skyline, and following the construction of her hull, the shafting and its supporting bearings were installed but her three propellers were fitted following her launching. The centre propeller was four-bladed, cast manganese bronze of 16ft 6in diameter that would be driven by her Parsons low-pressure exhaust turbine. The two outward turning, three-bladed wing propellers built up from cast steel hubs and bolted on bronze blades were 23ft 6in in diameter and would be driven by the *Titanic*'s steam reciprocating engines. The *Titanic*'s massive bulk would be steered by solid cast steel 'plate' rudder made up of six sections bolted together, with an overall length of 78ft 8in and 15ft 3in wide. Its total weight was just over 101 tons.

At the day of the launch on 31 May 1911, those attending the list of VIPs such as Lord Pirrie, J. Pierpont Morgan and Bruce Ismay, were present, but it was not such a grand affair as one might suppose. Instead the *Titanic* followed White Star policy of not being formally named or sent on its way with champagne, merely the trigger was released at the appointed time of 12.15 p.m. and her slipway mass of 24,000 tons with a pressure on the launching ways of 3 tons/in² took just sixty-two seconds to glide down the slipway and into the waters of the River Lagan to the accompaniment of some 100,000 onlookers cheering. It had taken the application of over 22 tons of tallow, engine oil and soft soap spread over the launching ways to enable the ship's huge hull to slide down the gradual slope to the river. As she became afloat for the first time, 160 tons of drag chains were pulled along and took up the strain to arrest the *Titanic*'s sternward momentum and bring her to a gradual halt. Tugs then took her alongside her fitting out berth and it was here that her two sets of four-cylinder, inverted double-acting, triple-expansion steam reciprocating engines were installed on to the bedplates. In addition to these there was also a massive Parsons turbine, twenty-four double-ended and five single-ended Scotch boilers, piping, plumbing wiring and auxiliaries. The boilers were arranged in six entirely independent and isolated boiler rooms, and the uptakes from these six boiler rooms ran into three funnels, the aftermost fourth being a dummy. Other fittings included fans, generators, steering gear, ovens, condensers, evaporators and the refrigeration plant. There was also the interior like panelling, chairs, paintings, palms, lifts and furnishings. For first-class passengers the *Titanic* boasted a squash racquet court, a Turkish bath, a fully equipped gymnasium, a swimming pool (the first afloat), Parisian-style cafés and libraries staffed by librarians. Indeed some suites offered on the *Titanic* had private promenade space at a cost of £870 during the high season. First-class passengers also enjoyed free meals that were served in the Jacobean-style dining room; however, to dine in the à la carte Louis XIV restaurant, panelled in French walnut, was extra. The propellers (q.v.) were fitted in the Thompson Graving Dock and the entire fitting out period lasted some ten months in all.

The *Titanic* was completed, and following trials in which she achieved some 21 knots, was handed over to the White Star Line on 2 April 1912, under the command of Captain Edward J. Smith. With a gross tonnage of 46,328, an overall length of 882ft 9in and a beam of 92ft 6in, she was the largest moving object that had ever been constructed by man.

She left Southampton on her maiden voyage to New York on 10 April 1912, and following calls at Cherbourg and Queenstown had a total capacity of 329 first-, 285 second- and 710 third-class passengers aboard. On the night of 14 April she collided with an iceberg and sank with the loss of some 1,522 lives – a disaster that sent shock waves around the world and has stimulated discussion and research ever since. The *Titanic* was three years in the making and at the cutting edge of Naval Architecture and Marine Engineering technology of the day, and the epitome of Edwardian grandeur afloat. That said, it took only two hours and twenty minutes for her complete destruction and its attendant loss of life!

Richard de Kerbrech
Gurnard, Isle of Wight

1

INTRODUCTION TO THE POWER PLANT

In a ship so large for its day, the *Titanic* (and also the *Olympic*), was driven by a combination of steam reciprocating engines and a turbine. These were overseen by a staff of twenty-two engineers and six electricians.

The main engines were very large, but not the largest as has previously been believed, and were twin four-cylinder, double-acting, triple-expansion steam reciprocating engines. The term 'reciprocating' denoted the nature of the motion of the engine parts upon which the steam acted, such as an up and down or a backward and forward motion. A simple steam double-acting reciprocating engine consisted of a steam cylinder inside which a piston moved up and down, according to the arrangement, a piston rod and a link or connecting rod worked a crank on a shaft which delivered the power for the work to be done. The reciprocating motion of the piston and piston rod was converted into rotary at the shaft by the crosshead and guide mechanism. Developments in single then compound (double) steam engines made more efficient use of the expansion of steam.

In 1911 with high steam pressures, the triple-expansion engine made further use of the properties of steam. The *Olympic* and *Titanic* had four cylinders arranged in line on the top of the engine structure, supported on columns. Each cylinder had two columns, 'forked' at the lower end, which rested on the base or sole plate carrying the shaft with four cranks, one for each cylinder. On *Titanic* and her sisters, the combined effect of lower weights and four cranks instead of three on each engine, helped reduce overall vibration. The piston rods passed out of the cylinder bottoms, the outer ends being guided between the columns to the crossheads, and the connecting rods joined up with the crankshaft. On the side of each cylinder there was a chamber for receiving or collecting the steam, ready for admitting it to the cylinder, and in these chambers there were special valves, worked by eccentric mechanisms from the crankshaft which admitted the steam and allowed it to escape at the correct instant.

These enormous engines worked on external combustion in which coal was burned in the boilers to generate steam from water which was then in effect, recycled. The pressure when all twenty-four boilers were in operation was 215psi, and this 'live' steam was supplied by the boilers via common steam main pipes which then travelled through the boiler rooms to the two main steam stop valves on the engine room side of the bulkhead. The main steam lines from the boilers also incorporated a bypass branch line known as the 'silent blow off' line. This could be used when warming through the main engines prior to start up, or as an emergency dump line for excess steam to a large exhaust to the condensers. Therefore if the engines were stopped, steam passed to the silent dump to prevent high-pressure exhaust steam venting off through the boilers' safety valves and up to the waste steam pipes to the funnels.

From the main steam stop valves the steam entered the high-pressure cylinders via the regulator valve (or throttle) on each engine and expanded

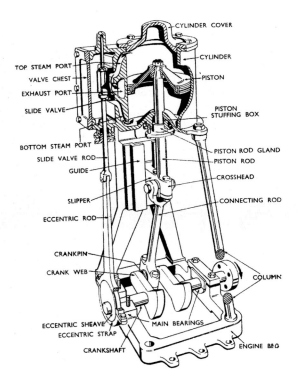

Cutaway detail of a single-cylinder steam reciprocating engine. (Author's collection)

The deserted stokehold of the *Aquitania* (1914) under coal. Note in the central front of the picture the firing rake or hoe, and to the right, a shovel hanging from a furnace door. The large lumps of coal had to be broken down into much smaller lumps before being fed into the furnace. (Author's collection)

The same view of the stokehold with the boiler grates being cleaned under the eye of a boiler-suited engineer, while the trimmer wheels his coal-laden barrow. (Author's collection)

The stokehold of the French liner *France*, completed in 1912. Note the coal piled by baffles to keep the passageway clear. The long handles hanging vertical are probably the damper levers to open the damper flaps located in the boiler uptakes. (French Line)

driving the piston down. Then it exhausted into the intermediate-pressure cylinder to do further work. As the steam expanded, each cylinder in turn was of a larger diameter or bore to accommodate the larger volume of the expanded steam. As the 'live' steam at high pressure was in turn used to expand through the three stage cylinders of her engines and converted the heat energy to mechanical energy, this in turn drove the ships two 38-ton, three-bladed outer propellers.

The expanded energy at this stage could not be used in a reciprocating engine properly because of cylinder size limitations. The combination of reciprocating engines together with a Parsons low-pressure (LP) turbine was first introduced by Harland & Wolff on White Star's *Laurentic* of 1909. It was found that the superior economy of the system was due to the fact that increased power was obtained with the same steam consumption by further expanding the exhaust steam at a much greater volume from the reciprocating machinery in the low-pressure turbine beyond the limits possible with the reciprocating engine.

The trials and operating experience of the *Laurentic* led to Harland & Wolff adopting the combination machinery for the 'Olympic'-class trio. The other option if manoeuvring or steaming at less than 15 knots, was the turbine could be bypassed by changeover valves which diverted the steam directly to the condensers.

Abaft of the main engines and on both sides of the LP turbine, were the condensers in which steam was condensed back into water and a vacuum formed.

In the 'open feed system', as it was known, after passing through the Parsons turbine, the now 'dead' or 'spent' steam then entered the two condensers, which had a combined cooling surface of $50,500ft^2$ and worked under a sub-atmospheric pressure of 28in. To condense the steam back to water, seawater at 60°F was circulated through nests of tubes by four compound steam driven centrifugal pumps with a suction and discharge pipe diameter of 29in. The steam was effectively condensed back into water to be used in the cycle over again. Dual air pumps on each condenser outlet sucked out the water and air, and it was pumped into two 2,790-gallon feed tanks. From these the condensate gravitated down to two 300-gallon capacity hotwell tanks. It was here that the condensate came into contact with the air, and any boiler water lost through steam leakage was made up with fresh water from the fore peak or from distilled water supplied by one of the *Titanic*'s three 60-ton capacity evaporators.

The water from the hotwells was drawn off by four hotwell extraction pumps, and to ensure that the feed water was free from oil and other impurities, was discharged through four main feed filters to the surface feed heater which was capable of dealing with 700,000lb/h (312.5 ton/h) of water when supplied with 50,000lb/h (22.3 ton/h) of exhaust steam from the generators at a pressure of 5psi. Thus the feed water temperature was raised from 70°F to 140°F. The water then passed to a direct-contact heater which could also handle a capacity of 700,000lb/h of feed water using exhaust steam from the auxiliaries such as the steering engines, the two refrigeration compressors, numerous pumps and windlass, the steam temperature was further raised to 212–230°F. After this the feed water then gravitated to four main feed pumps that returned the heated feed water back to the boilers above boiler pressure, to replenish and recycle the water back to steam once more. For continuous operation of the engines the rate of steam production in the boilers had to equal the rate of consumption.

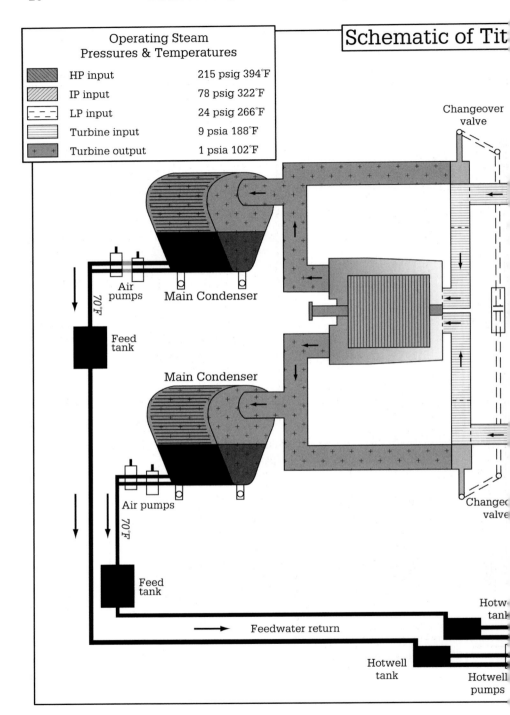

Operating Steam Pressures & Temperatures

HP input	215 psig	394°F
IP input	78 psig	322°F
LP input	24 psig	266°F
Turbine input	9 psia	188°F
Turbine output	1 psia	102°F

Schematic of Tit

Changeover valve

Main Condenser

Air pumps

Feed tank

70°F

Main Condenser

Air pumps

70°F

Feed tank

Changed valve

Feedwater return

Hotwe tank

Hotwell tank

Hotwell pumps

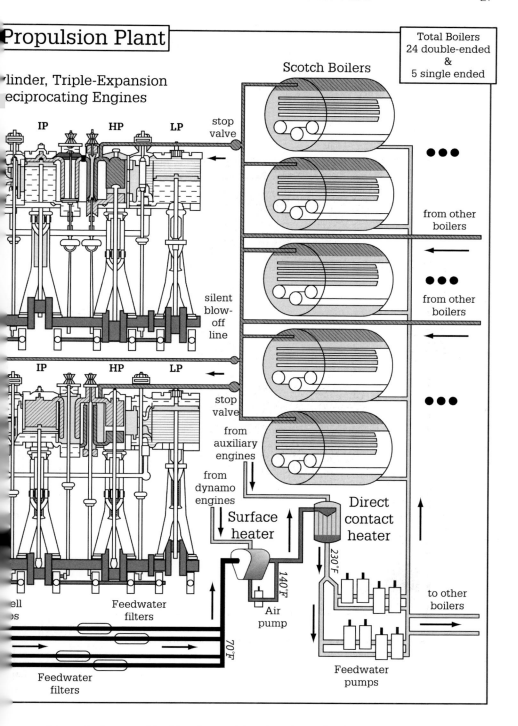

Schematic diagram of the *Titanic*'s propulsion plant. (Samuel Halpern)

2

ENGINE ROOM PERSONNEL, THEIR DUTIES AND ORIGINS

The following table gives the muster of engine and boiler room personnel – the Black Gang – which formed the major part of the engineering department aboard the *Titanic*.

Position	Number Signed On	Saved
Chief Engineer	1	0
Engineers	24	0
Electricians	6	0
Boilermaker	1	0
Junior Boilermaker	1	0
Plumber	1	0
Storekeepers	4	0
Leading Firemen	13	3
Greasers	33	4
Firemen/Stokers	161	44
Trimmers	72	19

Engineers

The engineers in 1912 were not considered as officers (for they wore no 'executive curl' on their sleeve insignia), and were responsible for the management and organisation of men in the engine and boiler rooms, together with the smooth, efficient and safe running of the boilers and main steam engines. In the engineer's structure, the chief engineer did not stand a watch but worked day-work and was in overall charge of the engineering department and its personnel. He was responsible for the safe and economical running of the engines, its fuel consumption and overseeing any breakdowns. In ships of the day his day probably started at 6 a.m. and before breakfast at 8 a.m. he had been round the bunkers to ascertain the amount of fuel remaining. This was a very important matter as it was uneconomical either to run short of coal or to have more than was reasonably necessary to complete the voyage. The former involved deviation to the nearest port to bunker; while the latter meant carrying coal bought, perhaps, in a port where it was more expensive than another port where it could be purchased cheaper.

In a ship as large as the *Titanic* the chief engineer would allocate about two hours' work to be done in the forenoon for writing up details of the ship's performance and keeping the top copy of the engine room log up to date. He would either take or delegate the third engineers of the watch to take 'indicator cards' to ascertain the indicated horsepower of the engines. He would also complete any records of any overhaul or adjustments that were made on the machinery.

About 11 a.m. he may well have had a meeting with the commander, the chief officer and doctor prior to any daily inspection of the ship. In this case the chief engineer's particular interest was in the auxiliary machinery throughout the ship, electric light fittings, etc., as the latter in a vessel of the *Titanic's* size were apt to be damaged if they were not closely watched.

For this massive responsibility the *Titanic's* Chief Engineer Mr Joseph Bell was the second highest paid man on the ship on £35 per month. This compared with the commander, Captain E.J. Smith, who was on a salary of £1,000 per annum!

In the structure there were six second engineers which meant two on each watch, one in charge of the engines and the other responsible for the boilers. There were five third engineers and a senior fourth engineer and this would have allowed for a further two certified engineers on each watch, most likely overseeing the boiler rooms. The remaining nine fourth, fifth and sixth engineers meant that another three engineers per watch could be allocated, giving a total of seven engineers to each watch at sea. This would have allowed for four engineers in the engine rooms overseeing the reciprocating engines, the LP turbine and other ancillary machinery such as pumps and also the steering gear, whilst three engineers would have been responsible for the boiler rooms. The senior most second engineer would likely to be on the four to eight watch, morning and afternoon. This enabled him to set the various day workers and to arrange with the storekeepers for the handing out of the stores necessary for the work that had to be done. All seconds on watch would determine the density of the water in the boilers by sampling the salinometer cocks and estimate the weight of ashes rejected from the furnaces.

There were two deck engineers who were on day work and were responsible for all deck machinery such as winches, capstans, and the windlass and lifeboat davits. Likewise the refrigeration engineer (extra fourth engineer) mainly oversaw the steam-driven refrigerating plant and covered the chilled spaces.

Electricians

There was at least one electrician on watch in the electrical engine room with its four steam-driven 400kW generators, with the remaining three, including the chief electrician, on day work. Their responsibility also covered all the electrical driven auxiliary machinery, lighting throughout the ship and navigational lights. (Oil- and paraffin-burning lights were the responsibility of the lamp trimmer.) The *Titanic* was installed with about 10,000 electric lamps ranging from 16 to 100 candle power!

Boilermaker and Assistant Boilermaker

Both time-served men, they were responsible for minor repairs on the boilers: replacing broken boiler gauge glass, seeing to leaking joints and leaking rivets, and also fire door hinges which were constantly in use. Both men were on day work and on call during watch hours. They were afforded junior engineer status and as such wore a thin braid ring on their tunic sleeves, edged with purple.

Plumber

Also with junior engineer status, the plumber was responsible for all the steam pipes which took steam from the boilers and the pipes that returned the feed water back to the boilers. He would also be called on to tend the domestic plumbing requirements throughout the ship. His pay was £9 a month, all found.

Storekeepers

At the top of the engine room, on both port and starboard sides, were flats which housed the engine room storerooms. In these were held various lubricants, including mineral, sperm oil and tallow grease. There were also brushes, asbestos packing for glands, rags, cotton waste, spanners, joint packing and boiler fittings. All these were in the safe custody of the storekeepers (who were equivalent to Royal Navy petty officer rank). They also oversaw the greasers' duties and their requirements, and were normally on day work starting at 6 a.m. and working through until 5 p.m.

Leading Firemen

Sometimes referred to as leading hand firemen, usually an older experienced man who more or less supervised the work of a gang of firemen to the satisfaction of the engineer of the watch on duty in the boiler room.

Firemen

The proper treatment of hand-fired, coal-burning furnaces was a skilled job, and the fireman or stoker who fed the boiler furnace played a very important part in the efficient steaming of a ship. The fires had to be kept evenly spread, about 4–6in thick; the coal had to be well broken up; clinker and dirt had to be raked out; and the furnace doors should not have been kept open too long. They tended three fires, two high and one low, and the task of keeping them at full blast demanded a good standard of physical fitness. In this event the fires had to be regularly and evenly fed, governed by the

Stokers at work aboard the USS *George Washington* in 1919. It was originally built in 1908 for the North German Lloyd and interred at New York until commandeered by the United States Navy in 1917. Note to left, the upper furnace door with air holes and the lower flap or damper of the ashpit. These sailors could well be conscripts. (US Naval Historical Centre)

reading on the pressure gauge and an eye on the water level. If they were sometimes (unwisely) stripped to the waist, sweat, burns and aching muscles were wreaked upon their bodies. Their pay was £6 a month, all found.

Greasers

Also referred to in other companies as oilers, these men worked in the engine rooms and shaft tunnels. They attended to the cleaning, oiling and greasing of the moving parts that involved sliding, oscillating and rotating machinery. Regularly filling the oil boxes and cups, the crossheads and slippers and the main crankshaft and tunnel shaft bearings. When in port and machinery was not moving or rotating, they ensured that lubricators were not operating and wicks or 'worsteds' were not siphoning oil from the oil boxes. Their pay was £6 10s a month, all found.

Trimmers

Originally from the title 'coal trimmers', they supplied the coal from the bunkers to the firemen and also carted away any ashes from the ashpits. One of their major duties in port was to 'coal ship'. Their pay was £5 10s a month, all found.

A more detailed account of the firemen's and trimmers' duties will be given in Chapter 5, Stokers, Pokers and Smokers.

Origins

In the early part of twentieth century British steamship companies, and especially those plying the North Atlantic, preferred drawing their firemen and trimmers from Liverpool-Irish stock. Although by all accounts fiery in temperament and 'bolshie' by nature, they measured up to the oner-ous tasks and got the job done. German steamship companies preferred Romanians and Hungarians.

So where did the *Titanic*'s firemen hail from? It is known that nearly 700 of her crew signed on at Southampton, just prior to her maiden voyage on 10 April 1912. These would also include firemen, greasers and trimmers of the Black Gang many of whom lived in the Northam district of South-ampton. On 29 March 1912, just prior to the *Titanic*'s builder's trials, origi-nally scheduled for 1 April 1912, a Belfast engine room crew of 182 fire-men, greasers and trimmers had signed on at Belfast, eighty-four of these had previously served on the *Olympic*. Their terms of engagement covered both the trials and the coastal voyage to Southampton and provided a pay-ment of 5s for each day the trials were postponed by inclement weather.

One might think that it was logical for those that undertook the coastal voyage from Belfast to Southampton would sign off and re-engage for the maiden voyage. But this was not the case and only seven who signed on at Belfast, two greasers, four firemen and one trimmer, agreed to continue working on board once they had reached Southampton! Were all those that signed on at Southampton on 6 April local to the town? It is believed that many of those who did were in lodgings, hostels or the Seamen's Mission in the port and it is possible that many were of Liverpool-Irish origin; some may even have married and set up homes with local ladies in the town.

Before sailing, firemen, greasers and trimmers signed Articles of Agreement at the shipping office when it was also customary to draw an advance note, besides which married men could opt to have a large part of their wages allotted to their wives and dependents ashore. Prior to the allotment system it had been known that some firemen pawned their best shoes while they were away so that their families had money for food. When they returned they used part of their pay-off wages to redeem their shoes. In passenger vessels like the *Olympic* and *Titanic* and good class vessels, probably 50 per cent of the stokehold crew would have continuous service, if not with the same ship then with the same company and it was no different with White Star. With respect to the firemen, except for the few needed for working a ship in port, they were paid off at the end of each voyage and were without pay until they signed on again for another voyage, either on the same ship or a different one.

In the early years of the twentieth century, conditions on board for engine room crew were indeed spartan and grim, and on many older ships firemen and trimmers had no designated changing or wash rooms, consequently they brought coal dust and sweaty grime into their accommodation from which few cleaned themselves before rolling exhausted into their bunks. It was extremely difficult to prevent such a space from becoming filthy and squalid. These spaces then took all the all-pervading smell of a mixture of body odour, coal fumes, cigarette and pipe tobacco smoke, oil and urine. On ships that carried grain such areas could become infested with cockroaches and rats. It is of interest to see how the Victorian author William John Gordon observed the conditions of the Black Gang in his 1896 book *The Way of the World at Sea* in which he wrote:

The crew of a large passenger ship is, nowadays, divided into three messes: the quartermasters, carpenters, and seamen dine in the forecastle; the lamp trimmers and stewards have their meals in the glory hole; and the stokers and greasers wherever they can get them, in the regions below. In some quarters, an effort has been made lately to improve the conditions under which the stokehold hands exist, but much remains to be done. To have no resting place but in a bunk, which has to hold not only your bed, such as it is, but also your clean clothes and dirty clothes; to eat your food with your fingers, and have no way of washing but in a bucket, to say nothing of the temperature and the grimy nature of the occupation, may have charms for many, but it is not a state of things to be hankered after. Of course, there is pay, and there is promotion, which, however, is not of extensive range. You join as a coal trimmer and are advanced to be fireman; when you are in port you are employed in the engine room, and thus become acquainted with the parts of the machinery, until the day arrives when you step up to be an 'oiler', as it is called in some lines, or 'greaser', as it is called in others. From a greaser you become a storekeeper, or donkeyman; and there is your career.

Of the stokehold and its environment Mr Gordon went on to observe:

The old stokers had a hot time of it, and some of them have now; but the introduction of closed stokeholds and closed ashpits have brought the temperature down considerably. The old plan was to trust the natural draught that came below through the intakes; the new, is either to pump air into the boiler room, or else to pump hot air direct on to the fire. Under the old plan, if there were not sufficient difference between the stokehold temperature and that of the external air, as in the Red Sea, for example, the fires would not burn; and they always burnt better when the vessel was steaming to windward. But under the new system, neither the position of the wind nor the temperature of the air makes any difference, for the draught is as much under control as that of a blast furnace.

Without such appliances, a stokehold is decidedly a warm place, and in the bigger ships life would be unendurable. When it is considered that some vessels are compelled to have 40 tons of coal alight at the same time in their furnaces to keep them going, it can be imagined what the temperature would be like if the draught were unaided. A stokehold is the only place afloat in which it is not obvious, at first glance, that one is on board a ship. Standing on the flagged floor, and looking at the boiler faces, no matter which way they may go — lengthways, crossways, or in groups — it seems as though one had strayed into the boiler room of some factory or colliery on a foggy day; and the resemblance is all the greater when the ship is in port and preparing to start in a day or two, and the men are in the cold furnaces, cleaning them out.

Mr Gordon painted an austere and gloomy picture of the Black Gang's world but his publication followed the Merchant Shipping Act 1894 in which their conditions were due for enhancement in that a Provision Scale was laid down for the officers and crew, albeit a minimum in the larger shipping companies. In this Act wage arrangements, accommodation and feeding for ships' crews was much improved, and by the time the *Titanic* entered service it could attract firemen and trimmers to those tasks, which were still onerous and physical but with a promise of designated quarters and better messing facilities. These will be dealt with in a later chapter. One of the surviving firemen, George Kemish, remarked about the *Titanic*:

> The *Titanic* was a brand new ship, and a grand ship too in those days ... Being such a fine new ship all the best ('cream') of Southampton seamen and Engine Room Department men were anxious to join her, yes the thick of So'ton went in her ... Being a new ship on her maiden voyage (everything clean) she was a good job in the stokehold. Not what we were accustomed to in other old ships – slogging our guts out and nearly roasted with the heat. Even so the *Titanic* would have burned over three thousand tons of coal on each trip.

There were no forced draught fans provided for the boilers but it had been the practice of the White Star Line to have forced ventilation only to the boiler rooms of their ships. For the latter purpose twelve Sirocco fans, two per boiler room, had been supplied by Messrs Davidson & Co. of Belfast, fitted with Allen motors.

While at sea under full steaming conditions, leading firemen, greasers, firemen and trimmers would maintain the watch system, eight to twelve; twelve to four; four to eight, both a.m. and p.m. and their accommodation was also arranged such that those on the same watch would be billeted on the same deck.

Firemen's and trimmers' welfare and concerns were represented by the National Sailors' & Firemen's Union (NSFU) and also by the breakaway British Seafarers' Union which was formed in Southampton on 6 October 1911.

3

COAL, BUNKERS AND BUNKERING

In the early part of the twentieth century the solid fossil fuel coal was truly King or King Coal as it was known. In the UK it heated the homes and factories, was the raw material for the generation of town gas in gas works that existed in most towns and cities nationwide; it was used in the nation's iron foundries, steelworks and coking plants and was also the fuel that drove the steam locomotives and steamships.

Coal consists of fossilised vegetable matter. The vegetation of past ages being buried in the earth undergoes compression and slow mineralisation; the first product is lignite, a coal which ranges in colour from yellow to dark brown, and is still rich in volatile constituents. Further mineralisation produces bituminous coal, a fuel which contains a large proportion of volatile matter. Anthracite is a coal produced by the elimination of the volatile constituents, and was the most perfectly mineralised coal we had in the UK. Semi-bituminous and semi–anthracite are coals intermediate in composition.

The principal constituents of coal are carbon, hydrogen and oxygen. The best of anthracite contain more than 90 per cent carbon; bituminous coal contains from 50 per cent to 60 per cent carbon and up to 30 per cent volatile matter. Semi-bituminous coals have proportions of carbon and volatile matter between these. The percentage of oxygen ranges from 1½ per cent in the best anthracite to 30 per cent or 40 per cent in the poorest lignite. Ash varies from 3 per cent in the highest classes of coal to 25 per cent or 30 per cent in the poorest.

The volatile matter in coal is composed chiefly of hydrocarbons. These make the coal easy to burn, and facilitate the production of flame. To burn hydrocarbons completely a high temperature and a plentiful supply of air

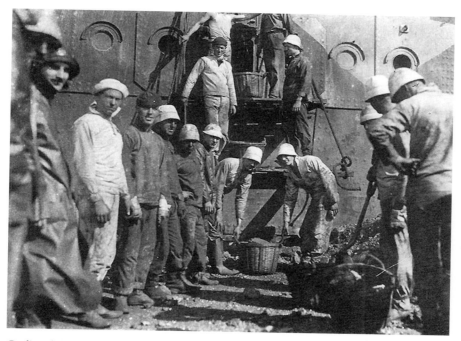

Coaling the USS *Leviathan* at Brest during 1918. The labour-intensive wicker baskets of coal are handled up to the coaling port. (US Naval Historical Centre)

are simultaneously required. Failure to secure these conditions with bituminous coal will cause black smoke to be formed. Much ash causes the furnaces to become dirty, and clinker may be formed by the fusing of the ash, with the consequent choking of the air spaces in the furnace. Sulphur in the coal is harmful to the furnace plates.

Anthracite is usually jet black in colour and is very clean. Sudden application of heat causes it to break up into small pieces. It is best worked with light fires and forced draught, and the furnace should be of ample capacity, as the heat is very intense. There is no smoke produced during combustion.

Semi-anthracite and semi-bituminous coals were much used for steam-raising purposes. The best Welsh coal contained just sufficient volatile matter to secure easy combustion without the production of black smoke. Other qualities required more care in the stoking to secure this result.

Bituminous coals were useful for the manufacture of 'town' gas for which purpose the large quantity of volatile matter present made them valuable.

Heating values or more technically referred to as Calorific Values, in British Thermal Units per pound (BTU/lb), of some of the solid fuels used in passenger liners of the day are tabulated thus:

FUEL	HEATING VALUE (BTU/lb of fuel)
Best Welsh coal	16,000
Average Newcastle coal	14,900
Average Derbyshire coal	13,900
Average Lancashire coal	13,900
Average Scotch coal	14,200

In the Royal Navy of day the best Welsh coal was designated as No 1 Welsh coal and was regarded as the world's best for marine boilers with the rest nowhere near it. There was also No 2 Welsh coal which produced slightly more soot and smoke. One of Welsh coal's drawbacks was its deterioration. This arose from two principal causes. The first was the oxidation of the organic constituents of the coal when exposed to air. This was known as the 'weathering of the coal', and was greatly intensified by increase of temperature. The second cause was the very friable nature of Welsh coal, which caused it to easily break up when handled.

Newcastle and Scotch coal burned much faster than Welsh coal, but did not give out such an intense local heat. With regard to Welsh coal there was little or no flame and very little smoke. Rarely were tongues of flame

USS *George Washington* bunkering at New York in November 1918. The use of mechanical coalers improved the time for a ship to be bunkered and turned around. (US Naval Historical Centre)

The *Olympic* alongside at the Ocean Dock, Southampton, coaling prior to her maiden voyage on 14 June 1911. The coal ports are open and the stages in place, with the coal barge moored between the quay and the ship. (Claes-Göran Wetterholm Archive)

seen licking in the furnace. The flame within the furnaces burned with a high intensity, appearing more like a bright incandescence cloud of vapour rushing from the top of the coals towards the rear of the furnaces. By the colour of the cloud of flame and the surface of the fire (in firemen's parlance the 'fire' was not the flames but the bed of incandescent coals upon the grates), the firemen could judge whether or not the coals had been spread properly and whether the fires required any additional working. If the surface of the fires had a bright, light yellow colour all over (around 2,000–2,200°F), the fires were of the correct thickness. When they burned with a reddish flame they were too thickly laid, and when laid too thinly, there was a tendency to burn holes through the bed of coals, made visible by a dull red flame surrounded by a white hot one.

At the time of the *Titanic* and her sister, British coal held its own as the best available bunkering fuel, because its chemical analysis showed it to be superior to coal available in any other part of the world. Coal bunkered in the United States was of the soft, bituminous type and had a high dust content.

As mentioned, steam coal is a semi-anthracite or semi-bituminous hard coal with a low ash content. White Star Line, as with other ship owners,

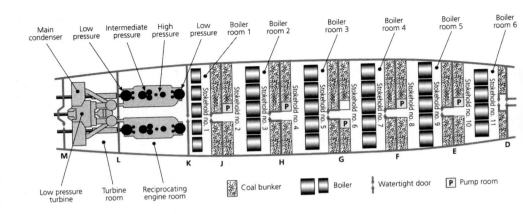

A plan showing the arrangement of the coal bunkers and stokeholds in the *Titanic's* boiler rooms. (Samuel Halpern/Matthew Marke)

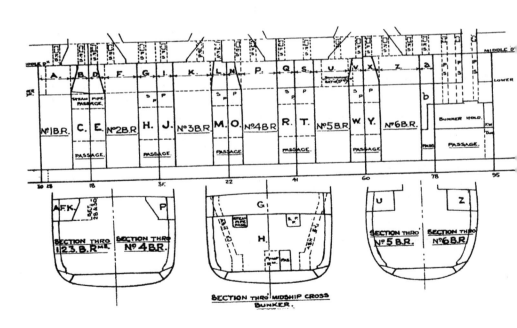

The *Titanic's* bunker layout, including sections through the boiler rooms, showing where the coal was stowed. (*Thomas Andrews' Notebook*)

having decided the best quality most suitable for their passenger vessels, had to take into consideration surrounding circumstances, such as the class of furnace, the natural draught, size of boilers, description and width of fire bars; the latter especially where mixtures of large and small coal might be burned. In addition the duration of the voyage and the facilities for bunkering thereon had to be considered. To get the best out of an average steam coal there would have to have been a fair draught, no excessive quantity of small coal, and most important, the boilers should have to have been of such a size and type, relative to the amount of steam required for the engines, that sufficient grate area and heating surface existed to allow for the production of the necessary steam without undue forcing of the fires. It was always necessary to avoid if possible coal so bituminous as to run on the fire bars and clog or burn them. The presence of slack (very small pieces of coal and dust) in bunker mixture was not necessarily detrimental to the general efficiency. Given certain conditions, the small coal, which was always present to some extent in a commercial delivery, by agglomerating and opening out as it did on the fire, and by the caking of the small and its expansion into a cellular condition by the heat of the fire, gave ready combustion and the passage of unburnt coal through the bars was prevented.

Ash in coal was always an impurity, some of which was intimately mixed with the coal, but in whatever form it occurred it was chemically and commercially valueless. If it formed clinker in the grate, it interfered with combustion, while if it formed running clinkers, it materially reduced the output of heat, in addition to damaging the grate or fire bars.

During combustion, ash was continually forming in the furnaces, and for its removal the furnace had to be raked out and the fire bed remade, which had a bad effect on the boiler and on the quantity of steam formed. Anything from 3 per cent to 20 per cent of the weight of coal might be left in the furnaces as ash, and fall into the ashpit. On steamships when the main engines were stopped the normal rate of steam production in the boilers should also stop, otherwise the steam pressure will rise, the safety valves lifted and the steam vented to the atmosphere. Coal fires cannot be extinguished, for the main engines might call for a supply of steam at any time. The situation was met by shutting off the air supply or draught, by either the ashpit dampers locally, or for a higher state of emergency the large damper flaps situated in the boiler uptakes at the base of the funnel. If the stoppage was likely to be a lengthy one it was effected by banking the fires.

A view from the deck of the USS *Leviathan* while bunkering at Brest during 1918. The swarm of stokers and ratings are shifting coal from the barge to the adjacent coal ports. (US Naval Historical Centre)

The coalminers' and transport workers' strike of 1912. While the coal strike was threatening, work proceeded night and day to collect a reserve supply for the Royal Navy. This view shows coal being unloaded for the fleet at Chatham. (Author's collection)

Bunkers and Bunkering

The *Titanic's* bunkers were fed through thirty-five port and starboard coaling ports just above F deck. Longitudinal or fore and aft bunkers ran between F and G decks but the coal was distributed throughout some thirty-four bunker spaces of varying capacities of which the eleven major bunker spaces were athwartships or transverse bunkers between G deck and the tank top and all held a total capacity of some 6,611 tons. All bar two port and starboard bunkers were identified by capital letters. The bunkers were constructed that the watertight bulkhead divided them such that each was shared by the boiler rooms. Through these bunker spaces ran the 'firemen's passage' slightly to starboard of amidships, with a watertight door at the aft access of each passage through the bunker. The steam pipe passage on both port and starboard sides also ran through the bunkers below the lower deck.

For bunkering or 'coaling ship' the coal was supplied to the *Titanic* by White Star Line's Southampton coal agents R. & J.H. Rea. Coal was transferred from (coal) colliers into barges with a capacity of between 500 and 1,000 tons, which were rowed alongside the *Titanic*. Prior to any loading into the bunkers every ventilator cowl was covered with canvas, any air vent louvers were closed and all interior spaces sealed off, and where possible access doors, port holes and companionways kept shut. The process of coaling ship was overseen by the chief engineer, who monitored the ship's list and trim as the coal was being loaded aboard and transferred within the bunker spaces. In the era prior to mechanical loading of coal it was shovelled from the barge into large quarter-ton buckets which were then hoisted up and tipped down the coal chutes into the bunkers. As mentioned, the coaling ports were just above F deck and were essentially openings in the shell plating with location lugs that could accommodate a two-man precarious steel platform or stage that protruded from the ship suspended each side by wire guy ropes, in conjunction with a temporary sheet iron scoop. In addition a row of simple derricks were rigged above, along the superstructure just below the promenade deck. These were hinged to the shell and swung out at right-angles when needed for coaling and swung in and secured against the hull when not in use. The coal buckets were hoisted up from the barges by a pulley block attached to the jib of each derrick and tipped into the port from which the coal cascaded down the chutes and landed in piles on the steel decks within the upper bunkers on the G deck level. In all there were some thirty-four bunker spaces and some six ports served each boiler room bunker.

Although many crew turned to to perform this onerous task, particularly for the trimmers as it came within their domain. Working as quickly as possible, the trimmers shovelled the incoming coal into wheelbarrows and wheeled (or sometimes dragged) the load to 'trimmers' openings' in the deck, located across the tops of the lower bunkers, where it was dumped down and evenly distributed. As the lower bunkers became full, the remaining coal was evenly distributed across the upper bunkers which surrounded each boiler room. They had little protection other than a wet rag tied over their face to keep the choking dust out of their lungs. The trimmers worked at this task in regular shifts from the time coaling ship began until its completion. This was a time-consuming, dirty and exhausting task, and by this method 12 to 15 tons of coal per hour were handled by a gang of six men, which could take from twenty-four to forty-eight hours to coal a vessel of the *Titanic's* size. It is not surprising therefore, to learn from past experience the crew hated this dirty and back-breaking job, or that the highest incidences of crew absenteeism were recorded amongst the trimmers.

The *Titanic's* coal ports were of a unique design constrained by the requirements of their location. As they were the lowest doors in the hull, any leakage through them would be serious and could lead to major flooding. Hence the doors of the ports had to be very strong and when closed and sealed had to be watertight and intrinsically safe as part of the hull. They had to withstand the buffeting from heavy seas, the ship's hogging and sagging stresses in a seaway and the impact of berthing and tugs. The port door plate was secured in the closed position by a heavy cast-steel brace or strongback, that spanned the inside of the door aperture when closed (in a similar fashion to a boiler manhole opening), in the vertical position. Integral with the strongback was a large diameter threaded steel stud that extended out from the strongback though a central hole in the door, outboard of the door was secured a large nut. When the nut was tightened (screwed up) the door was pulled tightly against the ship's plates. A buckram gasket soaked in red lead was located between the door and its aperture when closed to ensure a watertight seal. The coal port door was hinged such that it could be swung out and be completely clear of the opening when in use.

Before coaling the ship's carpenter went over the ship's side with a large spanner to slacken back the single strongback nut to each coaling port door, turned the nut and bolt such that the strongback was in the doors diagonal position, therefore unsecured and swinging the door outwards onto its hinge. Following bunkering the carpenter sealed up the ports with a buckram gasket that had been soaked in red lead, and also a hemp or buckram washer similarly red-leaded under the nut, prior to tightening up. In addition every railing, deck, companionway and passageway had to be cleaned thoroughly, to remove the all-pervading deposit of black coal dust that had seeped everywhere.

Wet coal had to be avoided because moisture sometimes caused a rapid generation of heat and gas, especially when the coal contained a considerable quantity of pyrites. As far as possible wet coal was not shipped and the coal was kept as dry as possible after it was in the bunkers. Ships were not coaled on rainy days if it could be avoided and the coaling port plates were replaced as soon as possible after coaling to prevent water entering the bunkers from the scuppers when the decks were being washed.

Danger of Fire in Bunkers

When coal was stored in the bunkers, especially when they were adjacent to the boilers, danger of fire always existed and the likelihood of spontaneous combustion was always present when the temperature was high.

When coal is exposed to air it rapidly absorbs oxygen and this oxidation produces heat. Coal, especially when it was freshly worked, gave off a gas known as 'marsh gas' (methane) which was combustible when the atmosphere contained certain percentages of gas, like 5½ per cent or 20 per cent. However, if the atmosphere contained 10 per cent of marsh gas, the mixture was highly explosive! Heat was produced when a chemical action took place and if the temperature reached 1,200°F, the ignition point of marsh gas, a fire broke out in the coal and generally this occurred in the centre of the coal in the bunker space.

The gas was lighter than air, so surface ventilation was necessary to carry it away, and whenever possible bunker lids or hatches were removed in fine weather to facilitate this. Spontaneous combustion was more likely to occur with small lumps of coal than with large, since smaller lumps presented a greater surface area to the air. Inferior coal was also likely to prove more troublesome than good quality coal, and as far as was possible the bunkers were worked out in the order in which the coal was supplied. In this way coal was prevented from remaining in the bunkers for an indefinite period.

Any electrical wires passing through the bunkers would have to be protected by metal conduit tubing in order to protect the wiring insulation, for if the latter was damaged, any subsequent sparking produced, would constitute a potential fire hazard.

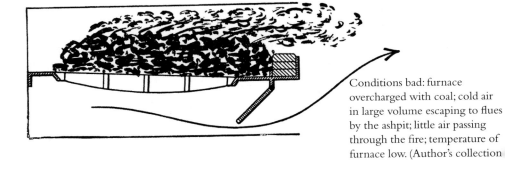

Conditions bad: furnace overcharged with coal; cold air in large volume escaping to flues by the ashpit; little air passing through the fire; temperature of furnace low. (Author's collection)

Conditions bad: cold air entering flues through hollow places without taking part in combustion of coal. (Author's collection)

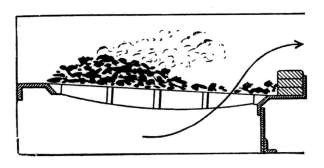

Conditions bad: fire looks well from front, but burnt out and hollow at back; cold air escaping to flue. (Author's collection)

Conditions good: air passing through fire to flues; maximum temperature of furnace; fuel incandescent; fresh fuel added in light charges; supplementary air supply through adjustable ashpit door for few minutes to burn smoke. (Author's collection)

Small bunker fires, if caught in time, were extinguished by means of sand which smothered the flame, but more serious, deeply seated fires had to be dug out if it was practicable and the burning coals removed completely. When water or steam was used to extinguish a bunker fire, large volumes had to be used otherwise 'water gas' was generated which in turn exacerbated an already dangerous situation. If it was at all possible the bunker space was sealed off completely to starve the fire of oxygen from the air; however, this operation had to be carried out thoroughly without any air leakage being allowed.

The *Titanic* would normally be bunkered with best Welsh coal or to be precise Lewis Merthyr Navigation Steam Coal and supplied by Lewis Merthyr Consolidated Collieries, Bute Docks, Cardiff in Wales. However, at the time she entered service there was a national coalminer's strike that ended on 6 April 1912 after some five weeks. The strike, in which nearly 1 million miners took part, caused considerable disruption to train and shipping schedules. Notwithstanding this, the *Titanic* sailed from Belfast with coal in very short supply but managed to load some 1,880 tons of her total capacity of 6,611 when she arrived in Southampton. The lack of coal was further aggravated by a smouldering fire in W bunker in No 10 stokehold on the starboard side of boiler room No 6, which ignited when she left Belfast. Often coal sluices down through which the coal passed into the bunkers, caused combustion, a conflagration easily extinguished by hoses. Notwithstanding this, Southampton's Board of Trade nautical surveyor, Maurice Harvey Clarke, granted her a Certificate of Seaworthiness. It was probably the largest ship he had to survey during his career to that date and he carried out three rigorous inspections. Even so, the unchecked fire smouldered on unabated for a further three days throughout her maiden voyage. Shortly after the *Titanic* departed from Southampton, the chief engineer ordered a gang of between eight to ten men, under the supervision of Leading Fireman Frederick Barrett, to empty the bunker and put out the fire, (this bunker had the capacity for 365 tons of coal). This was done by removing coal from the bunker and hosing down the burning coals. The huge pile of coal amassed on the plates and the extinguished coal was fed into the furnaces. It is believed that it was extinguished on Saturday 13 April on the 4 p.m. to 8 p.m. watch some seventy-two hours after the task commenced.

While at Southampton for the week the *Titanic* burned some 415 tons of coal to run the steam-driven generators and the domestic hot water and heating facilities. All that week in order that the *Titanic* should sail on her scheduled maiden voyage, coal was commandeered that was intended for other International Mercantile Marine Co. (IMMCo) ships, which included the *St Louis*, *New York* and *Philadelphia*. More coal was gleaned from other inbound White Star liners, the *Oceanic* and *Majestic*, which had bunkered extra coal in the United States. In all, some 4,427 tons were gathered from these vessels. It is probable that she may have been bunkered with an inferior quality coal in addition to the best Welsh that was normally supplied.

The fireman's task demanded a good standard of physical fitness, strength and stamina. (David L. Williams collection)

4

ABOUT SCOTCH BOILERS

Scotch boilers were the firemen and trimmers' stock-in-trade and the most imposing structures that they were acquainted with.

In its simplest form the Scotch boiler is a cylindrical, fire tube boiler, in which nests of tubes and support stays were mounted horizontally in a large drum-type vessel. Below these nests three large diameter furnaces were installed. The marine Scotch boiler was introduced in 1862 and from about 1870 onwards it became the most popular boiler in the British Merchant Navy. Its sturdy construction and reliability, together with its requirement for very little maintenance to keep it in good working order, initially made it suitable for pressures of 60psi and above. It came into its own when used originally in conjunction with the compound engine and it proved ideal for the long-haul cargo tramp steamers that eventually displaced the last generation of sailing ships. The Scotch boiler at the turn of the twentieth century was much favoured for marine use because of its robustness and the greater freedom which was taken in its operation. It was made in two forms, for firing from one or both ends, and known as the single and double-ended boiler respectively. In the latter the furnaces led in to a central combustion chamber. Double-ended boilers were used in preference to single-ended units where great powers were developed. One double-ended boiler cost less than two single-ended of the same total output, but the single-ended boiler required rather less upkeep and suffered less from local strains. A double-ended boiler had to be designed properly with regard to the brickwork in the combustion chamber, as it was possible for the firemen at one end to be injured by the flames back-firing when his colleague at the other end was stoking up. The Scotch boiler could be built with three or four furnaces.

Boiler – Technical Particulars

No. of double-ended boilers	24
No. of single-ended boilers	5
Diameter of all boilers	15ft 9in
Length of double-ended boilers	20ft
Length of single-ended boilers	11ft 9in
No. of furnaces on each double-ended boiler	6
No. of furnaces on each single-ended boiler	3
Total heating surface per double-ended boiler	5,702ft^2
Total grate area per double-ended boiler	130.8ft^2
Total heating surface per single-ended boiler	2,822ft^2
Total grate area per single-ended boiler	65.4ft^2
Ratio of heating surface to grate surface	43:1
Inside diameter of furnace corrugations	3ft 9in
Type of corrugation	Morison
Total no. of furnaces	159
Boiler working pressure	215psi (gauge)
Test pressure	430psi (gauge)

Steam for the *Titanic*'s engines was raised in twenty-four double-ended and five single-ended Cylindrical or Scotch boilers under natural draught conditions. Each double-ended boiler contained six furnaces (three at each end) while each single-ended contained three. When primed up each double-ended boiler contained 48½ tons (10,864 gallons) of fresh water.

In the Scotch boiler the coal burned in the furnaces which were all surrounded by water and the flames and heat generated was driven down to the combustion chambers. From here the hot flue gases rose to the upper part of the combustion chambers and passed through the nests of fire tubes, which were also surrounded by water, to the upper front of the boiler, which were then carried up the funnels via the smoke box and uptakes. The heat from the hot flue gases and the furnaces' exteriors was transferred into the water in the boiler and steam was generated. The water level was maintained at a height just above the top or 'crown' of the combustion chambers. Because the furnaces and combustion chamber were contained within the water space, of necessity the pressure vessel was of a large diameter. Construction of the Scotch marine boiler consisted of rolled mild steel plate 1⁴³⁄₆₄in in thickness with an Ultimate Tensile Strength (UTS) of 28–32 tons/in².

In the building of the Scotch boiler it was assembled by boilermakers using all riveted construction. The shells of the single-ended boilers were formed in a single ring, and those of the double-ended in three rings or cylindrical sections (each in two halves), joined by two treble-riveted double butt strap joints. The combustion chamber was riveted on to the furnaces, and the furnaces in turn on to the boiler fronts. The furnaces were flanged and riveted at the combustion chamber end and shaped for easy withdrawal through the front plates. In this manner renewal was assisted when required. The combustion chamber itself was held in position by stays attached to riveted brackets. All riveting was done when the rivets were red hot using the hydraulic (calliper) riveting machine which guaranteed the consistent quality of riveting. Limitations meant that this could only be used when the plates were accessible and could accommodate the calliper of the machine. However, when it came to completing the shell of the boiler, on one end of the double-ended boilers and the back end of the single-ended boilers a more manual process was involved. The ends were riveted in place like a giant lid, the flanges

A four-furnace boiler for the *Mauretania* under construction *c.*1906. The four horizontal furnaces and their combustion chambers to the left have been fitted to the furnace front. (Maurizio Eliseo collection)

themselves positioned inside the shell, and several positioning bolts were fitted through some of the rivet holes to keep them in place for riveting. The riveter with the 'holder on' dolly would be inside the boiler and hot rivets from the brazier passed through to him. These in turn would be placed through the aligned hole and held up with the dolly. Riveters outside the boiler would hammer it until the domed snap head shape was complete. After a double row of rivets had been completed the holder on craftsman would exit the boiler via a manhole door adjacent to the furnaces. According to Sennett and Oram's book, *The Marine Steam Engine*:

> In good boiler-making, the (riveted) joint should be tight without caulking; and if it be not fairly tight no amount of caulking will permanently remedy it, though it may conceal the defect for the time. Excessive caulking is very injurious, and it is probably one of the most fruitful cases of the grooving that sometimes occurs along the rivet seams.

Tubes and stays were later fixed when the shell was complete. Each double-ended was 15ft 9in diameter and 20ft long, while the single-ended boilers were 11ft 9in long. Inside the shell were three corrugated furnaces riveted at one end to a rectangular shaped combustion chamber. Three nests containing a total of 860 fire or smoke tubes of 2¾in outside diameter (430 in the single-ended) connected the combustion chamber to the boiler front, of these 284 were stay tubes. Water surrounded the whole of the furnaces, combustion chamber and tubes. Owing to the large flat surfaces of the boiler which were constantly under pressure, these flat surfaces were reinforced by eighteen longitudinal wrought-iron stays of 3in and 3¼in diameter between the end plates, and were secured by nuts on either side of the plates. Similar stays supported the bottom of the end plates and usually there were two stays around each manhole.

The plain tubes were expanded by means of a tapered swaging tool into the tube plate, with 256 of the tubes being thick-walled stay tubes screwed into both tube plates and 106 of them secured with a nut at one end.

Above left: A four-furnace, double-ended Scotch boiler under construction in Harland & Wolff's boiler shop during November 1898. Through the right-hand furnace aperture is a boiler destined for White Star's *Oceanic*. (Author's collection)

Below left: The boiler shop in the engineering department of Harland & Wolff, *c.*1901, showing three-furnace, single-ended Scotch boilers destined for Holland America Line's *Noordam*. (John McMillan)

The combustion chamber walls were supported by smaller stays of around 1¾in diameter at 7⅝in intervals. The combustion chamber top was supported by the chamber's walls, girders and stays.

The furnaces were made from 'Morison' pattern corrugated steel which had the following advantages whereby the strength was increased and the thin walled furnaces, of ⅝in thick, were good for heat conduction. The 'bellows action' of the corrugations prevented undue pull and stresses on the furnace fastenings during expansion and contraction. The corrugated profile gave an increased heating surface area compared to that of a plain surface. Each of the *Titanic*'s furnaces were of the Morison type of 3ft 9in diameter and fitted with fronts of the Downie 'boltless' pattern. These 'boltless' improved furnace fronts, as they were known, were designed to enable any of the removable parts of the flame plate or the door frame to be replaced quickly and simply without the use of tools as no bolts were used. They had been patented in 1906 by Messrs T. Downie and D. Brown and installed in White Star's vessels *Oceanic*, *Adriatic*, *Baltic*, *Celtic*, *Delphic* and *Laurentic*. They were of trapdoor style rather than swing door type. In the double-ended boilers' fire grate made up of separate replaceable firebars, was a firebrick bridge or baffle in the combustion chamber shared by the furnaces from opposite ends; in this way the fire was prevented from being pushed over into the common combustion chamber.

The boilers' working pressure were 215lb/in² (psi) but were hydraulically tested to a pressure of 430psi in accordance with Board of Trade (BoT) regulations. As a pressure vessel, the stress on a longitudinal seam was exactly double that on a circumferential seam. For this reason Scotch boilers were constructed with the longitudinal joints much stronger than the circumferential joints.

Although primarily a pressure vessel, the Scotch boiler had certain essential mountings like cocks and valves of which the minimum requirements were:

A water gauge: Probably the most important fitting which was never mounted directly on the boiler, but on a stand-pipe which was connected by a copper pipe at each end, with cocks mounted on the boiler shell at the top and bottom. The gauge itself consisted of a vertical glass tube, the ends of which were made steam-tight by stuffing boxes and glands at the ends of the gauge cocks mounted on the stand-pipe. The water in the tube showed the water level in the boiler. A drain cock below the lower gauge cock allowed the blowing through of either gauge cock with the

The boiler shop with furnaces and combustion chamber being built for the *Britannic*. It shows two vertical furnaces with their bellows–like corrugated structure, to increase its heat exchanging area, fixed either side of their common combustion chamber before being installed into its boiler shell. (UF&TM)

other turned off to make certain that neither end of the gauge was choked with scale or impurities, such that a false water level reading was indicated. It was generally best practice to mount gauges such that the lowest part of the glass was situated 4in above the combustion chambers' crowns.

Ordinary gauge glass burst occasionally, generally when the gauge was being blown through after the drain cock had been opened. Blowing down of the gauge was normally carried out once during each watch as standard procedure. One of the precautions taken by engineers performing this task was to turn their back on the gauge whilst manipulating the cocks in case the glass broke during this task and avoid glass pieces damaging their eyes. This task could be carried out from platform level by extended rods.

The double-ended Scotch boilers on the *Titanic* and her sisters had a water gauge integral with test cocks at each end of the boiler.

At least two safety valves on top of the shell: These were of very special design to ensure reliability. They were loaded by springs, and covered over to prevent their rise by more than a quarter of their diameter should a spring break. A long spindle terminated at the bottom in a coned end with a rounded point, the latter was a loose fit in a hole in the valve with a rounded bottom well below the flange on the valve which rested on the valve seat. Both valve and seat were flat, and the valves attached to the bottoms of the spindles by split pins. Means was provided for turning the valves to make sure they did not stick on their seats. Easing gear was also fitted by means of which the valves could be lifted from some position which was free from danger of scalding by steam. Long coiled springs of square-sectioned steel on the spindles held the valves down and only allowed them to rise and allow the escape of steam. This valve automatically opened when the boiler pressure exceeded the normal (i.e. 215psi), and allowed the steam to escape up the waste steam pipe on the funnel until the pressure had fallen again to normal.

Note on Safety Valves: These were of the spring-loaded, non-return type. A spring-loaded valve was a means of relieving the boiler from any excess of working pressure. It was large enough in diameter and had sufficient lift to allow the steam to escape as fast as it was generated when the pressure rose to a little over what the predetermined load had been set to, and also made to close again as soon as the pressure had dropped below that load. The valve should be self-acting and enclosed, so that it could not be tampered with and not effected by the motion of the ship. When a lip was formed on the valve and the correct area in accordance with predetermined calculations based on boiler working pressure complied with, a spring-loaded valve had very little disadvantage. A tamper-proof padlock was usually fitted to prevent interference by unauthorised personnel. A broken spring was usually a very rare occurrence.

One Main Steam Stop Valve: This valve was fitted to the top of each boiler and controlled the supply of steam to the main engines from the boiler. It consisted of a mushroom valve which was screwed down on to its seat by a spindle. The latter projected upwards through a stuffing box and gland, and had a square thread on which it could be screwed through a nut integral with a crossbar, which in turn was mounted on stanchions attached to the valve cover. The spindle was turned by a wheel or crossbar at its top.

Main Feed Check Valve: The feed water returning from the engines entered the boiler through this valve which was usually situated at the end of the boiler and admitted water just below the working water level, replenishing the water as steam was formed.

Auxiliary Feed Check Valve: This was always fitted as a standby valve in case of an accident to the other.

A Steam Pressure Gauge: Each boiler was fitted with a brass 'Bordon tube' pressure gauge which was connected by a copper pipe with a cock near the top of the boiler shell. The pipe dipped down into a 'U' bend below the gauge and usually became full of water by condensation. The steam never reached the gauge itself but indicated the pressure of steam generated in the boiler. (NB: The pressure indicated was always above atmospheric and known as 'gauge pressure', i.e. 'o' the zero was at atmospheric pressure.) A small sector (similar to a 'pie-chart' portion) on the gauge's white dial was painted red to indicate the maximum working pressure of the boiler. This bit of the gauge was dubbed by firemen 'the blood'.

A Salinometer Cock or Valve: This was used to draw off a sample of the boiler water for test purposes of the water's density, especially for the salt content in the boiler water.

A Scum Valve: These were fitted to the boiler shell with an internal pipe terminating with a pan (or dish) at the end which was just below the boiler water level. They were used to scum or cleanse the surface of the water from oil or other floating impurities. Care had to be taken to shut the valve before the water level dropped below the pan or dish, otherwise steam would be blown out.

Two rows of almost complete
double-ended Scotch boilers
for the *Olympic* in Harland
& Wolff's boiler shop. These
boilers, with their furnace fronts
mounted, were built by the
firm's workforce of boilermakers,
a now extinct trade. The figure
between the rows shows how
massive these structures were.
(UF&TM)

Three-furnace, double-ended Scotch boilers destined for the *Britannic* in Harland & Wolff's boiler shop. Below the nearest boiler is a stack of fire tubes, and just by them some boiler stays which supported the boilers internally. (David Hutchings collection)

A Blow Down Valve: This was used to blow out mud and scale and other heavy impurities and also to reduce the water level as required. It was situated near the bottom of the boiler and connected to a valve in the ship's side. The steam pressure in the boiler was used to blow the water out to sea through this valve.

A Circulating Valve: In the Scotch boiler, water in the upper part was apt to become much hotter than that at the bottom unless there was some form of circulation. To assist the process this valve was fitted to the boiler near its bottom and was only used to produce an artificial circulation of the water when raising steam. The circulators used on the *Titanic* were Ross-Schofield Boiler Circulators. This minimised stresses produced during unequal expansion of the boiler plates, and aided more effective heat transfer to the water.

Manholes: On double-ended boilers there was always one manhole at each end on the boiler shell at the top, to give access to the inside of the boiler above the furnaces, and one either side of the central furnaces at each end for access there. They were required for access during riveting, examination and repair. The holes were elliptical in shape and had their larger axis in a circumferential direction since a cylindrical shell was less weak circumferentially. They were closed by an elliptical door held in place by nuts and brass stays (dogs) outside the boiler. The doors were secured inside the boiler shell and the hole against which they were sealed was smaller than the door itself. By making the manholes elliptical in shape the door could only be passed through the hole on its smaller axis.

Even in Edwardian times it was rare that a boiler exploded. Most boiler failures referred to as explosions were the result of furnaces, smoke tubes or combustion chambers collapsing from external pressure through over-heating caused by loss of water or the presence of scale or dirt.

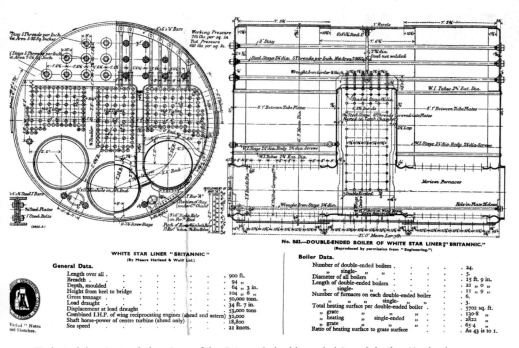

No. 883.—DOUBLE-ENDED BOILER OF WHITE STAR LINER "BRITANNIC."
(Reproduced by permission from "Engineering.")

WHITE STAR LINER "BRITANNIC"
(By Messrs Harland & Wolff Ltd.)

General Data.

Length over all .	. 900 ft.
Breadth .	. 94 „
Depth, moulded .	. 64 „ 3 in.
Height from keel to bridge .	. 104 „ 6 „
Gross tonnage .	. 50,000 tons.
Load draught .	. 34 ft. 7 in.
Displacement at load draught .	. 53,000 tons
Combined I.H.P. of wing reciprocating engines (ahead and astern)	32,000
Shaft horse-power of centre turbine (ahead only) .	. 18,800
Sea speed .	. 21 knots.

Boiler Data.

Number of double-ended boilers .	. 24.
„ single- „ .	. 5.
Diameter of all boilers .	. 15 ft. 9 in.
Length of double-ended boilers .	. 21 „ 0 „
„ single- „ .	. 11 „ 9 „
Number of furnaces on each double-ended boiler .	. 6.
„ „ single- „ .	. 3.
Total heating surface per double-ended boiler .	. 5702 sq. ft.
„ grate „ „ .	. 130·8 „
„ heating „ single-ended „ .	. 2822 „
„ grate „ „ .	. 65·4 „
Ratio of heating surface to grate surface .	. As 43 is to 1.

Technical drawing and elevations of the *Britannic*'s double-ended Scotch boiler. (Author's collection)

The empty shell of a single-ended Scotch boiler retained for ballast on the former Southampton tender *Calshot*. Although this boiler was built around 1928, it was of the same material and dimensions as those on the 'Olympic'-class. The furnaces and steam space stay nuts are still in place long after the boilers de-activication. (David L. Williams)

Common Defects to Scotch Boilers

Boiler defects would be encountered in boilers with some years' service behind them. Any running repairs could be carried out by the ship's boilermakers on board after first shutting down the boiler and taking it out of service. Dockside and repairs in drydock would be carried out during a routine maintenance period while shut down and drained. These repairs would be carried out by Harland & Wolff's shore side boilermakers.

When boilers were not in use they were not allowed to remain with their water at working level. The best practice was either to keep them 'pressed up' full after all the air was let out or to keep them empty and limed, with a heating stove to keep the chill off, particularly in cold weather. If the water was left in Scotch boilers and not kept pressed up, then the water level was changed daily.

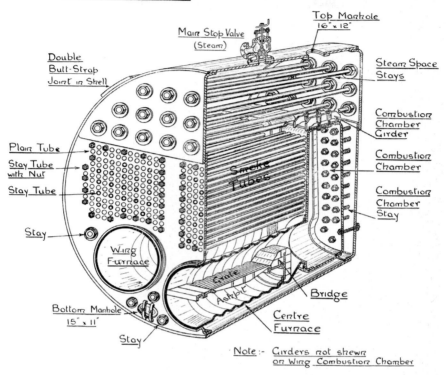

Cutaway drawing of a single-ended Scotch boiler showing the main parts used in its construction. (Author's collection)

Scaling and Cleaning

The enemies of efficient heat transfer were soot, a product of combustion on the inside of the fire tubes and scale on their water side. In addition scale on the inside of the plates and any oil in the water could deposit on the surface and cause 'hot spots'. (Any oil carried around by the condensate should have been filtered out by the feed water filters.)

When the boiler was empty, it was usually entered via the removed manhole covers. All steam and water valves were first screwed down shut by their spindles. Scale was then removed from the furnace and combustion chamber plates by chipping and scraping with care being taken not to damage the fire tubes. On fresh water boilers of the day, any scale formed would not have been too severe and all that was necessary to remove it was light scraping and wire-brushing. Any traces of oil on the shell plates,

This stokehold illustration shows transverse bunkers. Two firemen appear to be using a slice. In the foreground on the plates may be seen a slice and broom. To the right more slices are stowed in a rack with a pricker bar below, also the tap and hose can be discerned. Above are the forced ventilation shafts. (Hatchette Archive)

near the working water level were carefully removed. Oil deposited on plate surfaces during the blowing down process was removed and the plates washed with soda and water. Finally after descaling, the boiler water spaces were thoroughly washed down with a hose and all scale and dirt was removed by being raked out through the bottom manhole doors.

Sweeping of Tubes

The smoke or fire tubes were swept out by spiral-wound wire brushes screwed onto a long rod, which was pushed through each straight tube. The action was carried out during maintenance periods with the smoke-box doors removed. The cleaning of double-ended boilers was from the boiler front through to the combustion chamber. The soot and ashes were then removed from the furnace and combustion chamber and all burnt or broken firebars renewed.

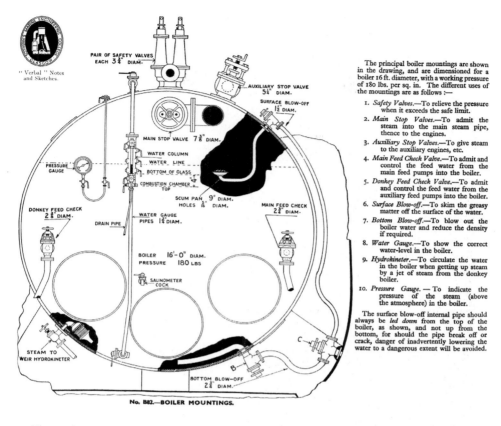

The principal boiler mountings are shown in the drawing, and are dimensioned for a boiler 16 ft. diameter, with a working pressure of 180 lbs. per sq. in. The different uses of the mountings are as follows :—

1. *Safety Valves.*—To relieve the pressure when it exceeds the safe limit.

2. *Main Stop Valves.*—To admit the steam into the main steam pipe, thence to the engines.

3. *Auxiliary Stop Valves.*—To give steam to the auxiliary engines, etc.

4. *Main Feed Check Valve.*—To admit and control the feed water from the main feed pumps into the boiler.

5. *Donkey Feed Check Valve.*—To admit and control the feed water from the auxiliary feed pumps into the boiler.

6. *Surface Blow-off.*—To skim the greasy matter off the surface of the water.

7. *Bottom Blow-off.*—To blow out the boiler water and reduce the density if required.

8. *Water Gauge.*—To show the correct water-level in the boiler.

9. *Hydrokineter.*—To circulate the water in the boiler when getting up steam by a jet of steam from the donkey boiler.

10. *Pressure Gauge.* — To indicate the pressure of the steam (above the atmosphere) in the boiler.

The surface blow-off internal pipe should always be *led down* from the top of the boiler, as shown, and not up from the bottom, for should the pipe break off or crack, danger of inadvertently lowering the water to a dangerous extent will be avoided.

The working end of a Scotch boiler showing its mountings. (Author's collection)

Repair of a Leaking Boiler Tube

Boiler tubes generally leaked at their back ends. They were repaired by re-expanding or by driving a tapered ferrule into the tube similar to that done with locomotive boiler tubes. Alternatively, the tube ends could be cut off flush with the back tube plate, and then driven through from the front end, following which they would be expanded. However, this was not considered good practice on ageing tubes. If scale was allowed to accumulate around the necks of the tubes, the water was prevented from getting to the metal, and the flame/flue gases passing through the tubes overheated them and tended to burn them away. Another factor which aided leakage was when cold air was admitted through the furnace doors. In this case the tubes, which were at a high temperature with the tube wall thickness much thinner than the tube plate, the tube contracted first which caused them to leak between the tube and the tube plate.

Repair of a Split Tube at Sea

In the case of a boiler tube splitting at sea it was necessary to be stopped entirely, but first the boiler fires had to be drawn down from the furnace belonging to the box of tubes in which the leaky tube was. A mild steel rod of the requisite length and about 1in diameter or so was threaded for 2in or 3in at each end, then inserted though the split tube. Two large washers were then turned with a rebate that entered each end of the tube with the larger diameter flush with the tube ends and with nuts on the threads. These were then tightened up to secure the washers and prevent water entering the boiler.

There were at the time special and patented tube stoppers that could be used if carried as a spare. One of these was Carney & Sevenoaks' patent stopper and Bedlam's patent stopper. The principle of these was the same as the improvised, bespoke one mentioned above.

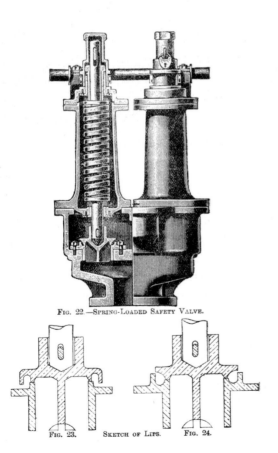

Fig. 22.—Spring-Loaded Safety Valve.

Fig. 23.   Sketch of Lips.   Fig. 24.

A spring-loaded safety valve similar to those used on the *Titanic*'s boilers. They would be set to lift at around 220–225psi. (Author's collection)

One of the *Britannic*'s 19½-ton boilers being slung and ready for lifting aboard and installing in the ship. (Maritime Quest)

After long periods in use the boiler gauge glass would become discoloured by scale or dirt, in which case they were replaced by new ones held as spares. More seriously, in time the glass being under constant pressure could break and shower those below with boiling water and steam. Hence urgent attention was required and the steam and water side were isolated by the cocks on the gauge, followed by repairs by the boilermaker.

Raising Steam

When lighting a Scotch boiler the boiler was first filled with clean fresh water to a level indicated by three-quarters of the gauge glass as this allowed for losses that may have occurred while warming through. Water was originally supplied by means of a hose from a shore side jetty or a water barge alongside. The fireman was then responsible for lighting or 'laying fires'.

The spider-like boiler uptakes for the *Olympic*, assembled in the boiler shop. These would have to be dismantled and refitted inside the ship. These structures contained the boiler dampers. (UF&TM)

The fire was usually lit in the centre furnace first. A quantity of kindling wood and rags soaked in paraffin oil was used as a normal accelerant. Firstly the furnace grate was covered with lumps of coal the size of a man's fist spread evenly over the grate to a uniform thickness of 4in. The portion of the grate halfway back from the furnace grate would then be 'wooded and topped', with care taken to keep fuel clear of the plates adjacent to the furnace door. When the fires were lit the boiler dampers and furnace door were open and the ashpit door and main steam stop valve shut.

With the oily rags and wood lit and the fire well under way, the fire would then be spread across the whole grate by a firing rake in order to cause ignition through the whole of the coal on the grate. The two adjacent furnaces were ignited by a shovel full of red-hot coals being placed on their coal covered fire bars. Alternatively, another common practice was to light the three furnaces together.

The furnace doors were then closed and the ashpit doors opened, the amount of opening was ultimately dependent upon the rate of combustion

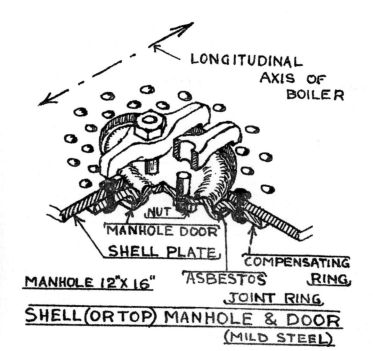

LONGITUDINAL
AXIS OF
BOILER

NUT
MANHOLE DOOR
SHELL PLATE
MANHOLE 12"X 16"   ASBESTOS
COMPENSATING
RING
JOINT RING
SHELL(OR TOP) MANHOLE & DOOR
(MILD STEEL)

A drawing of a manhole door used for access during construction, cleaning and maintenance of ships' boilers. (Author's collection)

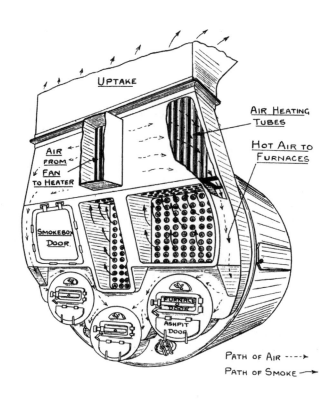

UPTAKE

AIR HEATING TUBES

HOT AIR TO FURNACES

AIR FROM FAN TO HEATER

SMOKEBOX DOOR.

FURNACE DOOR

ASHPIT DOOR

PATH OF AIR ---->
PATH OF SMOKE --->

A sketch of a much later Scotch boiler showing the smokebox and uptake in place, and the air and hot gases flow through it. The *Titanic*'s boilers worked under natural draught, using no forced draught fans or preheater air tubes. (Author's collection)

required, but were generally opened very slightly to begin with. If it was necessary to raise steam as quickly as possible, firewood would be placed over the grates and also at the furnace fronts for 'topping up'.

Heating the 48½ tons of water to boiling point and turn it into steam was an extremely slow process, taking from eighteen to twenty-four hours at the most, therefore twenty-four hours' notice was generally given to engineers before steam was available to turn the engines. On boilers such as the *Titanic's* they were very rigid structures, and should one part of it be raised to high temperature while the remainder was comparatively cold, high stresses were set up in the metal due to the unequal expansion of the plate, hence the water had to be heated gradually. Since heat from the furnaces rose, the water above the furnaces became heated while water below the furnaces and near the boiler bottom heated less readily and artificial circulation by the boiler circulators (q.v.) was resorted to. A steam-driven feed pump was started using steam from a small auxiliary or 'donkey' boiler for this purpose. The pump drew water out of the boiler through the circulating valve (q.v.) and returned it to the top part of the boiler through the auxiliary feed check valve, thus allowing the heated water above the furnaces to fall to the bottom and heat this part uniformly. When steam was generated this artificial circulation was stopped and the steam pressure was then generally raised to the normal working pressure of 215psi.

5

STOKERS, POKERS AND SMOKERS

Firemen's tools:

Ash Shovel: A 9ft-long shovel of light construction used for removing the burnt ashes and slag/clinker from the ashpit trays.

Devil or Devil's Claw: A two-pronged rake used for levelling the fires on the grate and withdrawing loosened clinkers.

Hose: Usually located alongside the boiler and connected to a water main.

Rake or Firing Hoe: A 10ft-long steel implement similar in appearance and construction to a garden hoe and used for raking out quantities of hot coals and clinker.

Shovel: Also known as a 'banjo'. This was the fireman's main tool for transferring the coal from the plates into the furnace mouth. It was of robust construction with a wooden shaft and handle, well balanced and held a normal shovel load of 11lb of coal.

Slice Bar: Also known as a 'tommy' or 'jumbo'. An extra long poker of 40lb weight for reaching the rear of the furnace bars, with a loop handle forged at one end and a point at the other. This was used to lift clinker, slag and caught cinders from the grates. The slice generally had its pointed end at right-angles to the main shaft, giving it a 'beak' appearance about 6in long; this was not only so that it could locate and track along the grates' grooves but also to clean the grate from a lower angle if the furnace was too high for the fireman.

Pricker Bar: A smaller poker of lighter weight to dislodge clinkers and slag from the underside of the grate and prise it down into the ashpit tray. Also used by the trimmer to break up large lumps of coal into manageable smaller lumps for the fireman's shovel.

US Navy stokers aboard the USS *Troy* (ex–*Minnesota*) during 1919. The men are in a confined boiler room, overwhelmed by piles of coal. The central stoker in bib and brace overalls is stoking a two-furnace boiler showing the critical size of his shovel ('banjo') as it enters the furnace aperture; not an easy task in a heavy seaway. (US Naval Historical Centre)

Completed stokehold of the Royal Mail Line's *Aragon* in June 1905. The 'Olympic'-class would have been fitted with furnace doors of a similar type. (Author's collection)

Hand rag or Canvas towel/cloths: For use when holding the banjo and slice bar to shield against heat from the furnace.

The *Titanic's* twenty-four double-ended boilers were labour intensive and for each four-hour watch there were fifty-three firemen, twenty-four trimmers and four leading firemen on duty. Each boiler room required four trimmers to cart the coal and carry ash to the ejectors, mainly because there were two stokeholds in each of these rooms, one forward and one aft and each stokehold in turn had two bunkers, one to port and the other to starboard. To feed the boiler, furnaces needed from eight to ten firemen. One fireman was responsible for working one end of a delegated double-ended boiler. Hence ten firemen were required in each boiler room from No 2 through to No 5 which contained five double-ended boilers in each. In boiler room No 6, where there were four double-ended boilers, only eight firemen were needed. Leading firemen supervised the personnel in the double-ended boiler rooms. The second engineer usually set the watches, and those engineers on duty entered the boiler room by a succession of steel ladders known as the 'fidley', and the Black Gang would enter from their accommodation above the forepeak via the spiral stair ladder and through the 'firemen's passage'. At times when some of these boilers were not lit, the supernumerary crew on the watch section would be detailed off to other duties such as cleaning machinery, etc.

The duties of the firemen were to keep the supply of coal to the furnaces and to maintain the rapid steam supply; this proved a physically demanding and exhausting job and required a lot more skill and vigilance that laymen gave them credit for.

When the ship was under full steaming conditions, to help harmonise the firemen's duty, a device known as Kilroy's Stoking Regulator in conjunction with Kilroy's Stoking Indicator was employed. The stoking regulator set the time that each furnace was required to be fired. It could be set to regulate the firing of the furnaces every eight, nine, ten, twelve, fifteen, twenty, twenty-five or thirty minutes, depending upon how much steam was needed and the number of boilers that were on stream at any time. The desired interval for firing was set by the engineer of the watch at the starting platform.

These stoking regulators controlled eleven stoking indicators in the stokeholds. The stoking indicator showed which of the three furnaces needed to be fired at a given end of the boiler at a given time. In each boiler room a gong on the indicator would sound at the required interval

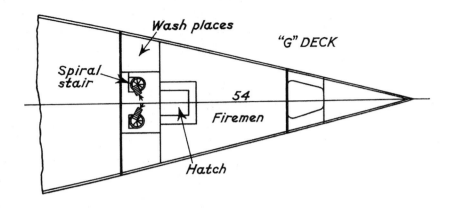

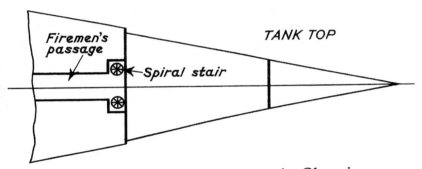

Firemen's quarters in **Olympic**

Above: Firemen were billeted together according to which watch they were on. Wash places were on the port side on each deck and lavatories on the starboard side. (Author's collection)

Left: Kilroy's Stoking Regulator and Kilroy's Stoking Indicator. A device to ensure the smooth and efficient stoking of the boilers in a constant rotational manner. Firemen and trimmers could hear its sound above the busy din in the stokeholds. (*The Shipbuilder*)

The stokehold of the *Aquitania* under coal-burning conditions. The trimmer in the foreground is emptying his barrow load of coal onto the plates. The fireman to the right is about to coal the near furnace, note how high he has to pitch his shovel load. He is assuming a legs apart stance. All men are wearing flat caps. (Author's collection)

and display the number of the furnace to be fired. When one considers the sheer noise in the boiler rooms it is not surprising that they required the additional audible alarm. For example, the normal cruising speed necessitated a setting of ten. A gong would echo though the stokeholds every ten minutes indicating the furnace to be fired; this signalled ten minutes for slicing, raking out and stoking. The next shrill of the gong marked the repetition of the cycle in another furnace. The lower the number of minutes selected by the duty engineer, the more relentless the pace, since the same series of operations had to be completed in a shorter time span. An experienced fireman could complete the tasks of the cycle within the allotted time span and give himself a welcome breather.

By having five indicators in each stokehold and one for each boiler, the timing could be staggered and coordinated so that the minimum number of furnace doors would be open at the same time, and no opposite doors on double-ended boilers open together. In this manner a systematic and regular rotation of firing was established.

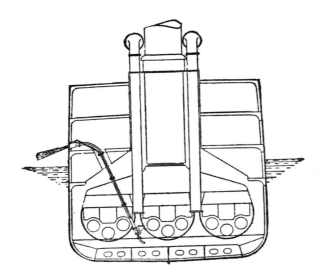

A sectional drawing of the general arrangement of See's Ash Ejector on a typical steamer of the day. (Author's collection)

The Kilroy's Stoking Regulator was independent of the main engine room telegraph but one can assume that the stoking work rate correlated with the telegraph demand. 'Full Speed Ahead' may well have required the regulator to display eight or nine. The boiler room telegraphs, which resembled a form of 'traffic light'-type indicator, were used to announce in advance what steaming conditions the engine room were anticipated in a relatively short period of time, for instance between the coming fifteen minutes to half an hour. Whereas the engine room telegraphs order communicated from the bridge, required an immediate action.

Generally as a vessel left or approached port, the revolutions were increased or decreased over a period of time and the bridge notified the engine room in advance of the anticipated changes of speed. Simultaneously the engine room would change the boiler room telegraphs in advance of any significant increase or decrease of the required firing rate. In response to this the firemen would alter the damper and ashpit door settings accordingly to increase or decrease the combustion rate in the furnaces and consequently the rate of steam generation. The advance notice was important to maintain the efficiency of the Scotch boilers, considering the volume of water they contained it took time to increase or decrease the rate at which the steam was generated. It was also important when one or more of the boiler rooms received the 'stop' order, sometimes towards the end of the ship's passage as the ship manoeuvred at a slower pace on her final approach to picking up a pilot and continuing on to berth or anchor. In the boiler rooms the 'stop' order did not necessarily mean 'finished' but rather it meant that regular firing was to be stopped, the damper and ashpit air doors partially closed, and the fires maintained in a 'banked' condition, by pushing to the rear of the grates in order to reduce generation of steam to a minimum and thus prevent loss of feed water through safety valves lifting and reduce stresses on the cooling boilers.

Firemen's and Trimmers' Duties

At the bottom of the engine room structure were the trimmers who worked in the hot airless bunkers where the gloomy atmosphere was thick with stifling coal dust. As previously mentioned one of their tasks was coaling the ship and spreading the coal throughout the bunker spaces. As the voyage progressed, they filled barrows with coal from the bunkers which was then tipped on the steel plate decking beneath the furnace mouths (separate from any raked clinkers). Also while at sea their

White Star historian, John Siggins holding his 9ft ash shovel from the *Olympic*. This was used for shovelling out lighter ashes from the ashpit tray under the grate of the furnace. They would be shovelled into a wheelbarrow and disposed of in the ash ejector. (John Siggins)

work in the bunkers continued using a miner's Davey safety lamp that was hung from a deck beam to cast some light into the gloom where their work was to move coal from the upper bunkers as coal in the lower bunkers was consumed during the voyage. Usually, in the main bunkers coal was cleared back towards the rear bulkheads, and in doing so they evenly spread and adjusted or 'trimmed' the piles of coal in the bunkers. At times the deck would be strewn with large lumps, and loads would be wheeled along narrow planks. Trimmers then had to trundle their barrows, known as 'being on the long run'. Of the twenty-four trimmers on duty per watch in boiler rooms Nos 2 to 6, ten of these were assigned to trim and transfer coal in the bunkers, the others, sometimes referred to as 'coal-passers', worked to and fro from the bunker doors in time with the firing rate, to replenish the coal pile of each fireman. The trimmers obtained coal from the doors in the cross bunker end bulkheads at the stokehold level, immediately opposite the furnaces. This arrangement reduced the handling of the fuel for each boiler to a minimum. When the bunkers were full, trimmers' duties were not so demanding as when the bunkers ran down towards the end of a voyage which involved a more laborious amount of shovelling to retrieve coal from the far end of the bunkers.

The trimmer upended his barrow next to where the fireman worked tending the furnaces. Under each double-ended boiler there were three furnaces at each end with a separate door. To conserve heat in the double-ended boilers, stoking was arranged so that doors were never opened at the same time (q.v.).

The fireman's task of keeping the furnaces at full blast demanded a good standard of physical fitness, strength and stamina. A fire in the firemen's parlance was not necessarily yellow flames licking from the coal but the orange and yellow glow of the coal emitting its maximum heat. The routine of tending a fire was exacting and had to be done in a specific order, at great speed, and with considerable strength.

During each firing cycle dictated by the Kilroy's Stoking Regulator, any clinker was dislodged with a 'slice' if necessary, the coals were levelled with the 'devil' to work the tops of the fire, after which four good shovel-fuls of coal were spread evenly over the top of the burning bed of fuel creating a carpet of coal between 4in to 6in thick. This task was completed as quickly as possible with the ashpit doors opened for as little time possible to prevent cold air from entering the furnace.

The above procedure is covered in some detail as it was standard practice to clean the fire of one of the furnaces in the six-furnace double-ended

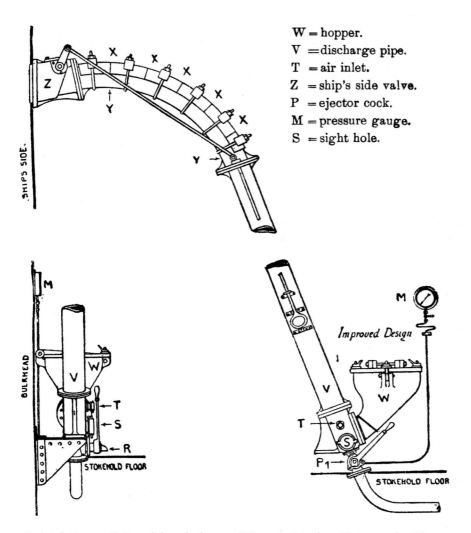

W = hopper.
V = discharge pipe.
T = air inlet.
Z = ship's side valve.
P = ejector cock.
M = pressure gauge.
S = sight hole.

See's Ash Ejector. (i) Open lid on the hopper (W) ensure it is clear. (ii) Open valve (Z) on ship's side via linkage handle and start duplex feed pump in adjoining room. (iii) Wait until gauge pressure (M) reaches 150psi. (iv) Open cock (P) near stokehold floor and continuously shovel ashes into the hopper. (Author's collection)

boiler towards the end of a four-hour watch, such that each furnace was cleaned every twenty-four hours which was a much more involved routine. (Royal Navy policy was to clean fires after 140lb of coal per square foot of grate had been burnt.) In addition an experienced fireman could judge by the appearance of the underside of the grates whether clinker (hard, white hot, fused lumps of slag and non-combustible impurities)

The stokehold was still a hot, dark, coal-dust ridden place to work, as endured by these stokers on the 1909-built Dutch ship SS *Hollandia*. Note the coal-strewn floor plates and a furnace door to the right marked 'To be cleaned'. In the bottom left-hand corner is the hopper of an ash ejector. (Denis Steele)

was formed on them, for these caused an obstruction to air for combustion. The first job was to clean out one of the furnaces which had already been prepared, by a process known as 'burning down'. Prior to this operation the damper above the furnace was closed sufficiently to bank the fire in the furnace to be worked on, and the ashpit door under the furnace closed. Any coal on the stokehold plates immediately in front of the furnaces to be cleaned was shovelled away from the area so that good coal would not become mixed up with burning clinker and lost. Firstly the coal above the clinker on the grate was pushed by means of a rake or 'firing hoe', above the opposite portion of the fire for the clinker to be removed. The fire bars were then cleared of clinkers, by lifting them then dislodged by a 'slice bar'. The 'tommy' was thrust home four times, once along each track of the grate, which showered ashes down into the ashpit tray and raised the clinkers to the top of the coals. The next operation was to rake these out in their white-hot state onto the plates by the firing rake, where they were quenched by hosing down with water. (This was avoided by letting the clinkers and cinders cool, otherwise a slurry of black sludge spread over the plates which could be slippery in rough weather.) The good burning coal was then pulled back from the opposite side of the fire to cover the portion that had been cleaned, and the process was then repeated for the other side. Another way of dislodging tenacious clinkers and cinders from the ashpit side was by means of a 'pricker bar', although thorough it meant that the ashpit door was open and there was a risk of hot sparks and cinders raining down on the fireman. Following this the grate coal was levelled up with the 'devil' and fired up with coal to the normal operating thickness before the damper was opened to give the correct amount of draught. The trimmers then shovelled out the fragments and raked out ashes that littered the deck into barrows. These were emptied into the See's Ash Ejector, or the 'blower', a receptacle connected to the side of the ship by a pipe through which water pressure at 150psi

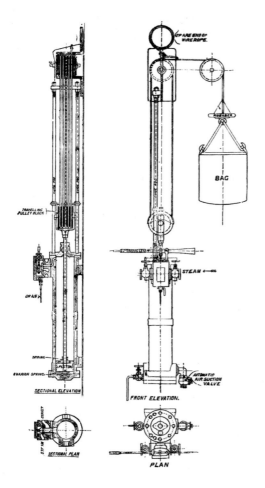

See's Ash Hoist. This manually operated device was used when the ship was in piloted waters or alongside in port. (Author's collection)

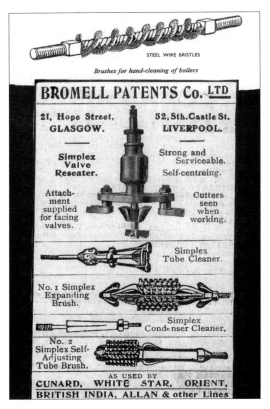

Brushes for cleaning boiler tubes
when the boiler is shut down.
(Author's collection)

forced or blew the waste material into the sea. This was known as 'shooting the ashes'. In order to expedite the task of removing ashes from the ashpit tray, the 'ash shovel' was used.

While the trimmers were disposing of the ashes, a fireman would be feeding a small amount of slack to the burned down furnace. This was known as 'coaling the bars', after which it was worked up to full capacity. In the meantime plenty of coal had been heaped onto the plates (separate to any raked clinkers or ash that may have accumulated there), when the firemen would begin stoking up, first making sure to adjust the draught lever before opening the furnace door. Failure to do this could result in a 'blowback', a searing hot flame shooting out across the stokehold. A 'pitch' of coal (about a dozen shovelful's or around 132lb of coal) was then thrown on each fire and the door slammed tight. This stoking up required a certain degree of precision, as the furnace door aperture was only just wider than the shovel or 'banjo'. If the edge of the banjo struck the rim of the furnace entrance during shovelling, it could cause a nasty jar to the fireman's arm or shoulder, besides shedding the coal. To prevent burns firemen used a

A scene from the 1958 film *A Night to Remember*. It shows the firemen raking coals in their white canvas rig in rather cramped conditions, while an engineer oversees the boiler room. (David Hutchings collection)

The *Titanic* departs Southampton on 10 April 1912, with the attending tug making a lot of smoke, its fireman having probably fed too much coal to her boiler. (Author's collection)

hand rag, piece of canvas or carpet. For speed opened the furnace doors with the blade of their shovel and then shut it with their shovel blade.

After the fire had burned for a while, a two-pronged rake or 'devil' was used for levelling off the spread of coal to an effective depth of 4in along the length of the grate. When clinkers formed they were removed by the heavy 'slice' under the burning coal, then lifting several times to assist combustion. Because of the length and weight of the 'jumbo', its point was sometimes raised by the fireman leaping up and down on the handle and bearing down with his stomach muscles!

When boilers were at full blast, maximum steam pressure was indicated on the brass pressure gauge above the fires with its needle pointing to the red zone on the gauge scale. This was called 'keeping her in the blood'. In addition, sufficient water in the boiler was constantly monitored by a watchful eye being kept on the water gauge glass level.

When the weather was rough, firemen learned to stoke as the ship's bow plunged down, slamming the door shut as the ship rose again to avoid a shower of red-hot coals on their feet. In a particularly bad gale, trimmers carried the coal in baskets rather than wheelbarrows and were usually able to keep pace with the reduced demand for steam. However, slow speed carried with it a guarantee of harder work when calm seas returned.

One of the *Titanic's* surviving firemen, George Kemish, recalled: 'Well being what I have called a good job – we just had to keep the furnaces full and not keep on working the fires with slice bars, pricker-bars and rakes.'

Ash Ejection

When fires had to be sliced or raked, the remnants of clinkers and ashes dropped into the ashpit tray below the grate from where air fanned the furnaces. Large ships like the *Titanic* consumed some 850 tons of coal each day which resulted, after burning, in around 100 tons of ash that had to be disposed of with the ship underway at sea (q.v.). For this See's Ash Ejectors were used, of which there were two in each of the large boiler rooms No 2 to No 6; ten in all recessed into the coal bunkers at various locations.

The ash ejector consisted of a large hopper into which ashes were shovelled and ejected over the ship's side though a pipe. The hopper was fitted with a hinged lid and grating to regulate the size of the clinkers before entering the hopper. The ejectors were worked by large duplex feed pumps adjoining each boiler room. The ashes were discharged by shovelling them into the hopper placed on the stokehold floor, where they were drawn down by the rush of air to a seawater jet at 150psi which was

The *Titanic* underway in The Solent. One of the few photographs taken by Cowes chemist and photographer, Frank Beken. Note the absence of smoke from the first three funnels, indicating the correct fuel/air mix. (Beken of Cowes)

discharged overboard via a long inclined pipe. It was in effect similar to flushing a toilet for ashes.

When the *Titanic* and *Olympic* were berthed alongside or in port approaches, the ash ejectors were not used for obvious reasons as no pilot cutter, passenger tender or shore side quay would wish to be showered with a thick black/grey slurry; indeed some port authorities permitted no ash dumping in their waters. For this purpose four Railton, Campbell & Crawford's steam assisted ash hoists were used instead and the ashes lifted up in canvas bags through a shaft and stored in rooms on E deck called the Ash Place. On the *Olympic* these were located amidships on the port side amid the stewards' and waiters' cabins and starboard amid the outside second-class cabins. The accumulated ash could either be disposed of by being transferred to barges alongside or unceremoniously dumped at sea after nightfall.

For working apparel, boots with peg leather soles or industrial clogs, as protection against red-hot debris underfoot, and dungarees (a coarse cloth originally made in the Indian village of Dungri) were worn down in the stokehold. In other prestigious companies canvas trousers and singlet vests would be worn. Often metal belt buckles on trousers were secured at the back as the buckle would become hot with the heat radiated from the furnaces. In general, all those who worked in the stokeholds wore flat caps (aka 'cheese cutter' or 'bunnet' by the Scots). This was to prevent coal dust getting in the sweaty hair and scalp causing it to become matted and dirty.

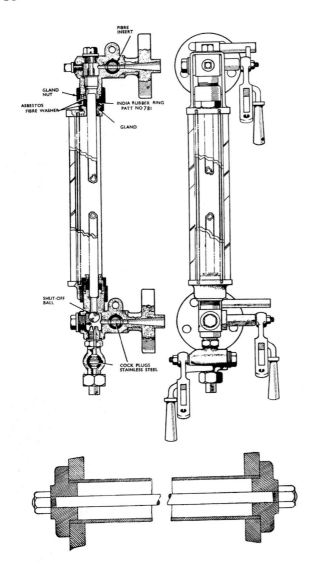

FIBRE
INSERT

GLAND
NUT

ASBESTOS
FIBRE WASHER

INDIA RUBBER RING
PATT NO 781

GLAND

SHUT-OFF
BALL

COCK PLUGS
STAINLESS STEEL

Top: A sectional drawing
of a boiler gauge glass.
(Author's collection)

Left: A common stopper
for a split boiler tube.
(Author's collection)

In the bunkers trimmers often wore only boots and 'long john' style draw-
ers, a cap and a wet rag covering their noses. Out on the plates the firemen
and trimmers wore a multi-purpose sweat-rag or bandana loosely around
the neck which was in constant use for wiping perspiration from face and
eyes and clearing lips and nostrils from a sticky, clogging accumulation of
sweat and coal dust.

To quench their perpetual thirst the stokehold gang drank from a large
can of oatmeal or honey water. If answering the call of nature became an
urgent necessity, a shovel was used with the furnace as a means of disposal

Thick reinforced glass surrounded the glass tube on No 25 gauge glass from the *Olympic*. (John Siggins)

The *Olympic's* No 25 gauge glass in its vertical position, the upper cock connected to the boiler's steam side. (John Siggins)

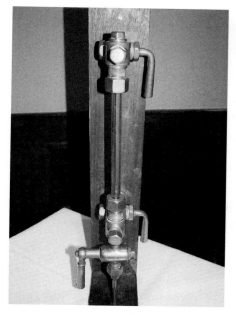

The *Olympic's* gauge glass. The off middle cock connected to the boiler's water side. (John Siggins)

The *Olympic's* gauge glass. The protective glass prior to mounting on the gauge. (John Siggins)

Above: The *Olympic's* gauge glass. The 'blind' nut at the very top of the gauge was for replacing glass tubes. (John Siggins)

Right: The *Olympic's* gauge glass. The lowest cock was for blowing down the glass tube and removing any impurities which obstructed the water level. (John Siggins)

(a most hygienic method if nothing else, human defacement having combustible properties).

For ships that plied the tropics the temperature could reach even higher to 140°F–150°F, and in the fierce scorching glare of the fires a man could be overcome by heat exhaustion, but soon recovered after a spell on deck. Even on the North Atlantic run, after a stint on each four-hour watch, bodies were dehydrated, faces and chests (if exposed) seared by the radiation from the open furnaces and hands inflamed from the heat of the 'slice bar' that penetrated through the double layer of canvas used as a mitt. Any burns and scalds to the skin sustained on duty were smeared with tannic ointment. Quite apart from this there was the shear noise level from the stokehold; that of scraping shovels on the plates, the crunching of coal under feet, the roar of air through ashpit doors, the clanging of furnace doors and the relentless peal of Kilroy's Indicator Gong.

On the 'Olympic'-class ships the firemen and trimmers were billeted separately. Originally the firemen were accommodated with 108 right forward on D deck, seventy-two trimmers on E deck, fifty-three firemen on F deck and fifteen leading firemen and thirty greasers on G deck. Each cohort of firemen and trimmers were grouped according to watches to avoid any disruption to off duty engine room crew and thus avoid any friction, e.g. twenty-four trimmers per dormitory. The firemen's mess was on C deck starboard, adjacent to the smaller greasers' mess and they were waited on by the firemen's messman or the greasers' 'peggy'. Each deck of accommodation had its own set of wash rooms where firemen had to do their ablutions and wash their own 'dhobi', and WCs. Here after the watch the Black Gang could use their sweat rags as flannels and then wring out for use as drying off towels. Food in the mess was adequate and plentiful, there being the usual condensed milk, tea, coffee, cocoa, sugar, butter, cheese and jam issued regularly. In addition sausages, sometimes tough meat, potatoes, haricot beans, hard dried peas, and lumpy rice or tapioca pudding could be on the menu. By maritime law the crew's menu in ships on foreign articles, which included those plying the Atlantic, had to include at least twice weekly a stodgy plum pudding nicknamed 'Board of Trade duff' or 'Figgy duff'. Whatever the meal, the Black Gang would consume copious amounts of salt to replace that which had been sweated out on watch below. There was also the entitlement of a drink of Board of Trade Fortified Lime Juice, issued on demand to all British merchant seamen, its bitter citric taste with 'a kick like a mule'. This gave them extra vitamin C and helped prevent scurvy; also it is believed that it repressed the sexual desire!

On liners like the *Titanic* the Black Gang off the 4 p.m. to 8 p.m. watch fared somewhat better, as trays of unconsumed food from the first-class dinner and saloon galley were taken forward every evening by the firemen's messman or greasers' 'peggy'. This treat was known as 'black pan' and there was a particularly plentiful supply of it after a spell of rough weather. Alcoholic beverages such as beer and stout were not permitted. That said, apparently between certain latitudes on either side of the equator the Black Gang were issued with a tot of rum at midday. The following account back in 1894 by a fireman by the name of Thomas McCarthy (judging by the name, possibly a Liverpudlian), indicates that alcohol may have been allowed under extenuating circumstances, even on smaller merchant ships seems to bear this out:

There were no trimmers on that ship. There were six firemen, and they reckoned to have two firemen on a watch; still, as there was no trimmer, they put one fireman on to the six fires, and one man had to go and trim. They put the six fires on the top of one man. They took two hours at the fires and two hours trimming. I have seen us come up the ladder so exhausted that we had to take the hand-rag in one hand and the sweat-rag in the other to get us up the ladder, it was so hot. Even though we signed no grog allowance, they knew the work was so exhausting that they gave us grog both going on and coming off, in leaving London and getting back. I believe that if we had not got that grog some of us would not have come back. For instance, at 12 o'clock, after the watch from 8 till 12, I have seen us lie down on deck and pant just the same as a whale out of water; lying down for 20 minutes fairly exhausted before we could take a bit of grub.

As for smoking, as strange as it may seem, it is thought that as was the growing popularity in Edwardian days, the smoking of cigarettes or pipes was permitted in the engine and boiler rooms by the staff therein, long before health and safety concerns were ever considered.

As previously mentioned, in the burning of coal in the furnaces, insufficient air or inferior quality coal would result in poor combustion leading to the production of black smoke emanating from the funnels which caused soot and smuts to land on the after and poop decks to the detriment of passengers in those areas. This could also occur by incomplete combustion that might have come about by blocked fire bars or incorrect adjustment of the damper flap. Smoke was usually caused by an excess of coal being thrown on the fire at one time. When coal was fired in thin light charges, the heat of the furnace was usually sufficient to prevent smoke, especially if a supplementary air supply was admitted over the fire for just such a period as the smoke was being given off. The fireman's main object was to obtain the highest possible temperature in the furnace, and to maintain as steadily as possible this condition of high temperature, there would be less smoke made because no fireman would then surcharge and smother his fires with black coal. Where this was done, it was a proof that the fires had been allowed to burn too low before re-charging. The presence of black smoke had a more sinister indication during the First World War as it was a signal to roaming German U-boats that a steamer was in the vicinity ripe for torpedoing. Examination of any of the photographs of the *Titanic* underway show that there was very little and in most cases no black smoke emanating from her first three funnels. Notwithstanding the fact that she was a brand new ship with new boilers, clearly the Black Gang demonstrated their hard-earned skills.

6

MAIN PROPULSION MACHINERY

Steam Reciprocating Engines-Technical Particulars

Diameter (bore) of cylinders:	54in, 84in, 97in, 97in
Stroke:	75in
Type of valves fitted:	Piston valves on HP and IP cylinders
Type of valve gear:	Stephenson link motion
Type of piston rings fitted:	Lockwood & Carlisle on all cylinders pistons, except HP and on all piston valves. The HP rings were of the Ramsbottom type
Diameter of HP and IP piston rods (high-tensile steel):	14in
Diameter of LP piston rods:	11¾in
Diameter of HP and IP connecting rods:	From 13½in to 15in
Diameter of LP connecting rods:	From 11½in to 13in
Diameter and length of top ends (HP and LP):	16½in by 17¼in
Diameter and length of top ends (LP):	13½in by 14¼in
Diameter of crank pins:	27¾in with 9in hole
Length of crank pins (HP and IP):	35in
Length of crank pins (LP):	24in
Diameter of crankshaft:	27in with 9in hole

A fireman could be promoted to a greaser and as such was responsible for the lubrication by oiling and greasing the main engines' moving parts and

A young man, possibly an apprentice, inside the *Olympic*'s port intermediate cylinder casting. (*The Shipbuilder*)

rotating, oscillating and sliding machinery. In the main this would involve topping up the oil boxes and oil cups of bearings at regular intervals, also maintaining the 'worsteds' or wicks in the oil boxes. They had to be pretty agile and keep their wits about them during the filling and top up of the oil cups on the main bearings and eccentric straps with the engines full under-way, for one slip or fall into machinery rotating at 85rev/min could lead to a serious injury or death! In addition, he would also attend to the lubrica-tion of auxiliary machinery and the shaft tunnel bearings. When not doing these there were oil leaks to attend to, general cleaning and as time went on painting main engine structure and support columns. All these duties were

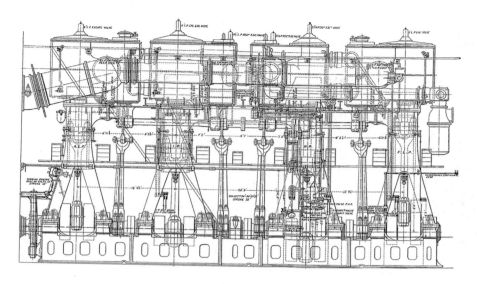

Side elevation of the *Britannic*'s main engine showing part of the main cranks and the eccentrics. (*The Engineer*, courtesy of Simon Mills)

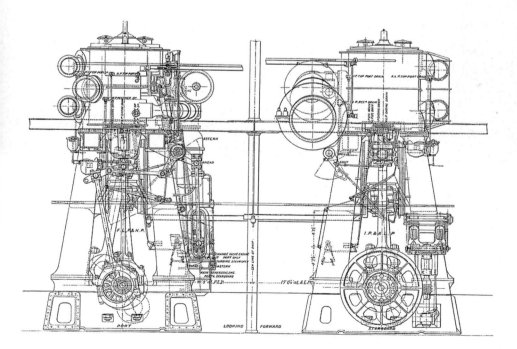

End elevation of the *Britannic*'s main engine looking forward. The array of levers and linkages looks complicated. The left-hand sectional view shows the Brown's reversing engine and the Stephenson's Reversing Gear's weighshaft. (*The Engineer*, courtesy of Simon Mills)

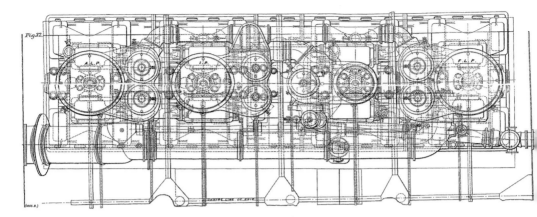

A plan of *Britannic's* port main engine. All cylinders (unlike on the *Olympic* and *Titanic*), except the high-pressure one show the dual piston valves adjacent to the cylinders. (*The Engineer*, courtesy of Simon Mills)

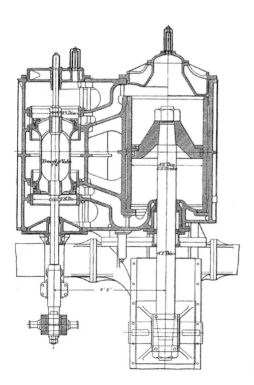

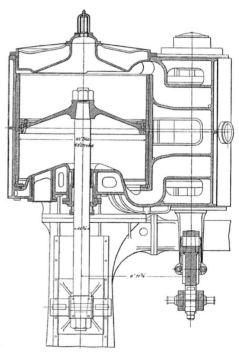

A section through the *Britannic's* high-pressure cylinder (right), with its adjacent piston valve (left). (*The Engineer*, courtesy of Simon Mills)

A section through the *Britannic's* intermediate-pressure cylinder (left) with one of its piston valves (right). (*The Engineer*, courtesy of Simon Mills)

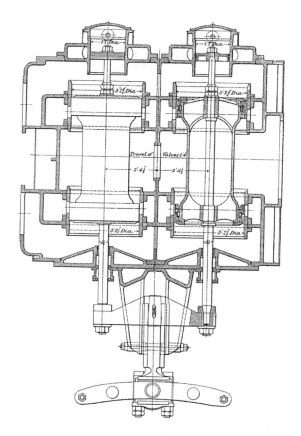

A section through one of
the *Britannic's* low-pressure
piston valves which worked
in tandem. (*The Engineer*,
courtesy of Simon Mills)

carried out under the supervision of the engineer on watch. This may seem
a strange progression from fireman but for regular Black Gang returners to
White Star they learned of the workings of the main engines at the other
end of the steam they had helped generate. Although less dirty and hot than
the stokehold spaces, the work was nonetheless demanding and one had
to be vigilant and wary, nipping in and around the moving machinery to
lubricate the rotating and sliding parts. Greasers could always be called on in
the case of an emergency or severe shortage to return to the stokehold and
augment the firemen there if necessary. This move was not very popular,
as the progression to greaser was seen as a further step up the engine room
structure. Little wonder that the stokehold could attract greasers to step up
to leading firemen when the vacancies arose without a significant increase
in wages. Even then these posts were not readily filled except by men with
families or dependants (or perhaps those men who may have fallen into
gambling debts or drink dependency).

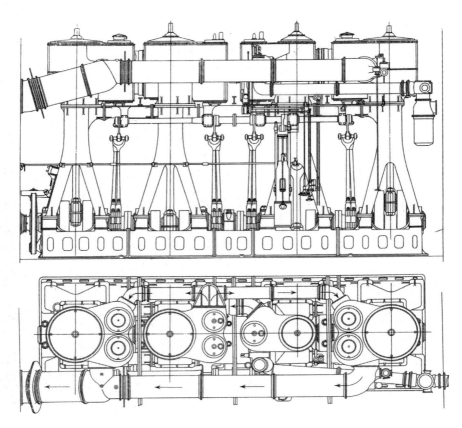

Profile and plan view of the *Olympic*'s four-crank, triple-expansion engine. The large LP cylinders are at both ends. In between the support columns are the ahead and astern connecting rods that were driven by eccentrics on the main crankshaft. (Author's collection)

The move into the engine room must have seemed like another world without the coal-dust laden atmosphere and the searing dry heat that hit the back of the throat when one entered the stokeholds. Instead of the constant scraping of shovels and the roar of furnaces, there was the sound of steam pushing the great pistons down their cylinders and the rhythmic 'swash, swash, swash' of the massive rotating crankshafts.

The *Titanic*'s marine engineers were mainly drawn originally, with few exceptions, from time-served fitters and fitter-turners in Harland & Wolff's shipyard. After a sea-going period an engineer could progress up the engine room career structure by the acquisition by examination of Board of Trade Second and First Class Certificates of Competency, and watch-keeping experience gained during sea service. Their principal

A scene from *A Night to Remember* of greasers in the engine room overseen by the second engineer. This was filmed at Metropolitan Water Board's Cricklewood pumping station. The engineer is sporting an 'executive curl' on his sleeve insignia; this would not be the case as only the navigators would wear this. (David Hutchings collection)

function was to oversee the efficient and safe running of their boiler rooms and engine rooms along with its auxiliary machinery. They ensured that the continued operation of the main power plant, along with any necessary lubrication and attendant maintenance of running machinery, ran efficiently and without interruption.

Any large breakdown like a broken connecting rod or 'wiped' white metal bearing, could be repaired at sea with the provision of the requisite spare parts; however, larger breakdowns, like a cracked or sheared crank-shaft or the shedding of a propeller blade, required repairs to be carried out by Harland & Wolff shore side staff at Belfast or Southampton.

As has previously been mentioned, they were not the largest marine steam reciprocating engines in the world but, along with the *Olympic* and

Britannic, were the largest ever built in the British Isles and possibly the most powerful. At some 30ft in height a 6ft-tall man could stand upright inside the cylinders at bottom dead centre, and standing in the middle of the piston crown would not be able to touch the cylinder walls of the intermediate and low-pressure chambers with outstretched arms! (Maintenance personnel would be called upon to enter the cylinders during overhaul to examine the bores for wear by taking diameter measurements with internal micrometers and extensions.)

The *Titanic*'s combination machinery (q.v.) was arranged as the plan of the triple-expansion engine layout shown below:

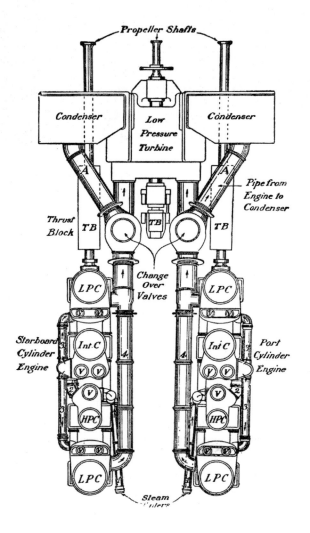

Layout of the triple-expansion engines and the exhaust (LP) turbine, which drove the three screws on the 'Olympic'-class. This combination machinery had been trialled in White Star's *Laurentic* of 1909. (Author's collection)

The *Titanic*'s starboard (to left) and port (right) main engines under construction. In the bottom right-hand corner may be seen the piston valves, 'D' slide valves and cylinder covers ready for assembly. (John McMillan)

In its simplest form the steam expansion engine works by steam entering the first cylinder through the stop valve and passes from it into the second and then into the two third cylinders. As the steam loses power as it goes on, the cylinders are larger the farther they are from the source of the steam. Inside each cylinder was a piston head fitting tightly into the cylinder bore. These piston heads were connected to piston rods that passed through steam-tight flanges at the bottom of the cylinders and extended down to where they were connected to the propeller shaft by crank webs that worked with a pedalling movement and turned the propeller shaft, known at this part as the crankshaft. As the steam passed from cylinder to cylinder it repeated this movement, each piston was bigger than the one preceding because the steam, being weaker, worked at a lower pressure and more of it was required to force down the piston head. For each cylinder, steam from the boilers was admitted to the high-pressure cylinder (HPC), and then the exhaust steam from these was led via steam slide valve gear to the intermediate or medium-pressure cylinder (Int. C), then from here the

End view of the port main engine under construction. It shows the LP cylinder and beneath in the toothed flywheel with steam-assisted turning gear disengaged. In the foreground are what appear to be two eccentric sheaves prior to fitting. The Harland & Wolff employee to the right gives some idea of the massive size of the engine. (David Hutchings collection)

steam was exhausted via steam slide valve into two low-pressure cylinders (LPC) at either end of the engine. As the pressure decreased the volume of the steam increased, hence the increase in cylinder bore diameters from 54, 84 and 97in and accordingly the increase in cylinder volume.

Typical state of the steam at these stages were as follows:

HP Inlet 215psi 394°F
IP Inlet 78psi 322°F
LP Inlet 24psi 266°F
Turbine Inlet 9psi(abs) 188°F
Turbine Outlet 1psi(abs) 102°F

From the two LP cylinders, steam at sub-atmospheric pressure passed to the Parsons exhaust turbine (aka the low-pressure turbine) on the central propeller shaft, where steam further passed through it before finally exhausting into the condenser to be turned back into water for recirculation via extraction pumps and feed pumps back to the boilers.

From the plan it may be seen that the steam from the main triple-expansion engines could either be led to the turbine or it could be directed straight to the condensers via large 'changeover' valves, thus effectively 'short-circuiting' the LP turbine. This latter operation would normally be done upon entering or leaving port or under similar conditions in confined waters where the *Titanic* had to be manoeuvred like a twin-screw vessel. The exhaust turbine would be engaged when she was 'full away' on passage in the open sea.

Titanic's main engines were balanced on the Yarrow, Schlick & Tweedy system whereby vibration of the main crankshafts during rotation was minimised by the crank angles and sequence being staggered. Considering the port engine, looking forward with anti-clockwise rotation, starting with the HP piston at top dead centre (TDC) the following sequence took place. HP at TDC then 106° for the IP piston to be at TDC, then 100° for the forward LP cylinder to be at TDC followed by a further 54° for the after LP to arrive at TDC, and finally 100° to bring the HP piston back to TDC (see p.96).

To get some idea of the terms and major components used in reciprocating machinery a generic section through a low-pressure cylinder of a steam reciprocating steam engine is shown overleaf.

Major machinery failures that required repairs to be carried out by Harland and Wolff's shore-side engineers when in the UK or the ship's

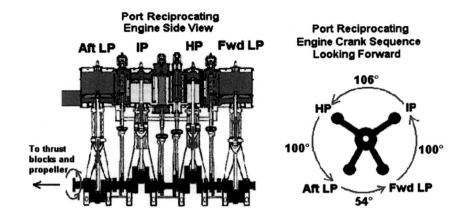

Schematic sketch of the *Titanic*'s main crank angles. (Samuel Halpern)

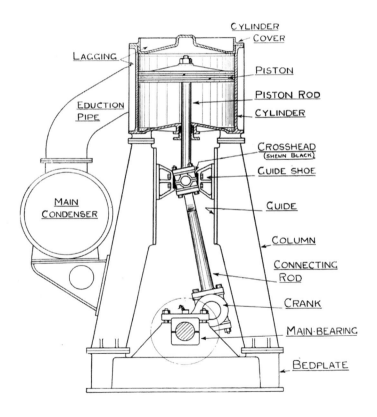

Diagram of an LP cylinder to clarify the engineering terminology. The piston shown is without its integral steam chest piston valve. As with the *Titanic*, the main crosshead link is between two guide shoes and also the piston is a conical shape. (Author's collection)

The *Britannic's* port main engine under construction. At the base of the engine are the half shells of the white metal journal bearings. (MaritimeQuest)

engineers when in the United States were: a broken connecting rod; cracked main piston; broken piston rings; cracked/sheared crankshaft; main bearing wiped; crosshead bearings wiped; leaking glands.

Mechanism of a Slide Valve

As the *Titanic's* main engines were double-acting, i.e. steam would expand and push the piston down towards the crankshaft and following this steam would be admitted to the underside of the piston to drive it back up. To enable this and change over the steam distribution, a mechanism called a slide valve was used which was timed, controlled and driven from the main crankshaft by an eccentric strap. (Eccentric whereby the slide/piston valves drive crank was offset from the centre of the main engine crankshaft.) On the *Titanic's* mains the HP cylinder was provided with a single piston valve and the IP cylinder with two piston valves, similarly operated to the twin slide valves on the LP cylinders. In these cases the twin valve push rods were joined to a common yoke driven by a central connecting rod from the Stephenson's Link Motion; the reversing gear for each set was operated by a Brown engine such that the valves could be repositioned when it was desired to manoeuvre astern.

The *Britannic's* completed port main engine with its starboard one, each weighing nearly 1,000 tons. This would be the sight engineers would have as they entered the engine room through the 'fidley' ladders. To the right are the engines being built for Holland America's *Statendam*. (National Museums Northern Ireland)

The slide valves used on the *Titanic's* HP and IP cylinders were of the piston valve type. As its name implies the piston had the form of a piston with two lands. As the steam pressure acted all round the valve it was self-balancing.

Piston type Slide Valve Operation (A Generic Description)

Starting with the HP cylinder which worked on 'inside steam admission'. When the piston commenced on its downward stroke and the piston valve was moving upwards, it just started admitting steam to the cylinder on top of the main HP piston with a pressure of 210psi. Steam then exhausted from the bottom of the cylinder under the piston over the lower land of the piston valve, via pipes to the IP valve chest. In this manner steam was supplied from the centre chamber of the piston casting through an upper port and exhausted at a pressure of 78psi via a port uncovered by the slide valve's lower land (see p.101).

The installation of the engines into the *Britannic*. An end of a crankshaft is in place on the engine room bedplates. Main bearings are in place and the open flat plates show where the main engine support columns will be located. On the stairs is the dark bowler-hatted figure of the foreman overseeing the outfitting. (MaritimeQuest)

Secondly the IP cylinder which worked on 'outside steam admission'. At the IP cylinder the two valves, one for supplied steam one for exhaust, were similar to that of the HP cylinder except that steam was on the outside of the valve and entered through a piston central chamber. Conversely the exhaust through the ports was controlled by the piston valve's lower land. A larger diameter exhaust pipe then led the expanded steam to the LP cylinders at the forward and after ends of the main engines (see p.101).

For the LP cylinders at the forward and after ends of the main engine piston valves were not used. If they had have been they would have required a large diameter or an increased length. Instead slide or 'D' valves were used for the much lower pressure would not have tended to force the valve casting away from its running face against the cylinder exterior.

In the case of these, the slide valves were in a steam chest casting integral with the side of the LP cylinder. The valve was a flat plate ('D' in section) which was recessed on the face towards the cylinder to form a rectangular

The built-up cranks of the *Britannic*'s engines, with a man alongside for scale. (MaritimeQuest)

cavity. The valve, as has already been mentioned, was driven from the main crankshaft by means of an eccentric which gave it a reciprocating motion over the flat running face of the steam chest with three slots cast in it. The upper and lower slots connected with the top and bottom of the cylinder and were known as 'steam ports', while the middle slot led to the exhaust pipe at the side of the cylinder and was known as the 'exhaust port' (E). Steam was admitted to the steam valve chest at 'S' where the steam pipe from the IP was connected, and could only enter the cylinder when the steam port at either end was uncovered by the slide valve.

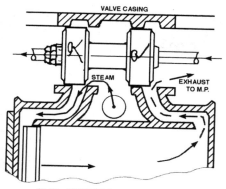

H.P. PISTON VALVE
(Inside Steam)
Piston leaving top centre.
Valve just opening to top steam,
and exhausting bottom steam.
Ahead eccentric follows the crank.

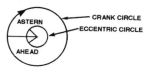

Diagram of operation of a high-pressure
(HP) piston valve. (Author's collection)

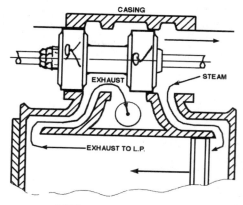

M.P. PISTON VALVE
(Outside Steam)
Ahead eccentric leads the crank.

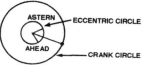

Diagram of operation of an intermediate-
pressure (IP) piston valve. (Author's collection)

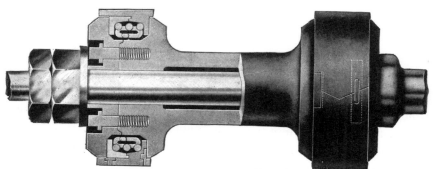

Photo by permission of Messrs. Lockwood & Carlisle

A later type of piston valve as used on locomotives, showing its own sealing rings for steam
tightness. (Author's collection)

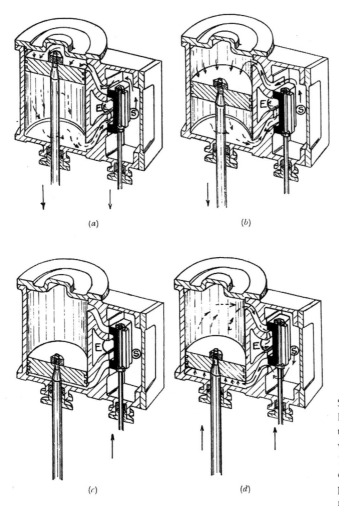

(a)   (b)

(c)   (d)

Slide valve operation. Four sketches showing the operation of a 'D' valve. The *Olympic* and *Titanic* had this type controlling their LP pistons, the *Britannic* did not. (Author's collection)

Referring to the diagrams it can be seen that:

The valve in (a) is moving downward, operated by the engine itself, and has partly uncovered the top steam port. Steam is flowing from the steam chest into the cylinder and is pushing the piston downwards, while the spent steam from the previous stroke is escaping through the lower steam port to the exhaust port via the cavity in the valve, as indicated by the dotted arrows.

In this diagram (b) the piston has reached half stroke on its way down, but the valve is in its extreme lower position (due to the setting of the eccentric drive in relation to the main crankshaft). The ports are fully open and steam is still entering the cylinder above the piston and continues to do so until the valve returns to its mid position as in diagram (c) and closes both steam ports.

The piston has now reached the bottom of its stroke and further upward movement of the slide valve opens the lower steam port to steam, which now enters the bottom of the cylinder and starts to push the piston upwards as in diagram (d).

Simultaneously the upper edge of the cavity in the valve uncovers the upper steam port and provides a passage through the valve to the exhaust port, by means of which the spent steam above the piston escapes from the cylinder to the exhaust pipe. In the case of this generic description it will be seen that this valve has admitted steam to the cylinder for the period of the complete stroke and no expansion of the steam has been permitted. It was possible to 'cut off' the admission of steam earlier in the stroke and make use of the expansive quality of the steam, in which the case the valve would be modified accordingly, but this simple type of valve will suffice for illustrative purposes.

Reversing Mechanism and Procedure (see p. 104)

As previously stated, the piston and slide valves received their reciprocating motion from the eccentric drives integral with the main crankshaft. There were two eccentrics that operated each piston/slide valve, one for ahead motion and one for astern. In simpler terms for description, the eccentric connecting rods were attached at their top ends to a slotted quadrant, which formed the basis of the Stephenson's Link motion. When the slotted quadrant was moved to the position shown in the left-hand diagram, the ahead eccentric was brought into line with the valve spindle. The ahead eccentric rod was thus in control of the valve. The astern eccentric at the same time idly moved the end of the link up and down.

Rotation in the opposite direction was effected by moving the link right over as shown in the middle diagram in which the astern eccentric controlled the movement of the piston/slide valve. In the right-hand diagram the link is shown in a position midway between the ahead and astern positions. In this position the movement of the ahead end of the link cancelled the movement of the astern end. The up and down movement of the valve would be very slight and not enough to drive the engine.

Although the slotted link mechanism has been described and illustrated, this movement mainly applied to smaller marine steam engines. In much

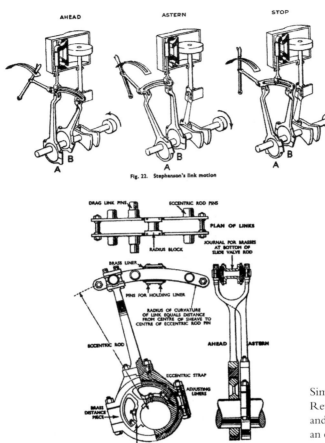

AHEAD   ASTERN   STOP

Fig. 22. Stephenson's link motion

DRAG LINK PINS   ECCENTRIC ROD PINS

PLAN OF LINKS

RADIUS BLOCK   JOURNAL FOR BRASSES AT BOTTOM OF SLIDE VALVE ROD

BRASS LINER

PINS FOR HOLDING LINER

RADIUS OF CURVATURE OF LINK EQUALS DISTANCE FROM CENTRE OF SHEAVE TO CENTRE OF ECCENTRIC ROD PIN

ECCENTRIC ROD   AHEAD   ASTERN

ECCENTRIC STRAP

ADJUSTING LINERS

BRASS DISTANCE PIECE

SHEAVE IN HALVES

Fig. 23. Eccentrics and links—details

Simplified Stephenson's Reversing Link operation and below a diagram of an eccentric con-rod and curved beam. (Author's collection)

larger engines such as the *Titanic*'s the slotted quadrant link was replaced by large parallel beams that were curved to the correct radius, similar in pattern to the illustration shown.

A block with a journal at the centre for the lower end of the valve spindle, slid between the curved beams which were held together by distance pieces at the ends. Short spindles near the ends of the beams were forged on them and formed journals for the forked upper ends of the eccentric rods. Also integral with the curved beams were the drag link pins. These pins were for linking up with the controls of the Brown's reversing engine situated on the inboard side of each main engine.

Brown's Combined Steam & Hydraulic Reversing Gear, to give it its correct name, consisted of a steam cylinder below and a controlling hydraulic cylinder above, with a piston rod common to both cylinders.

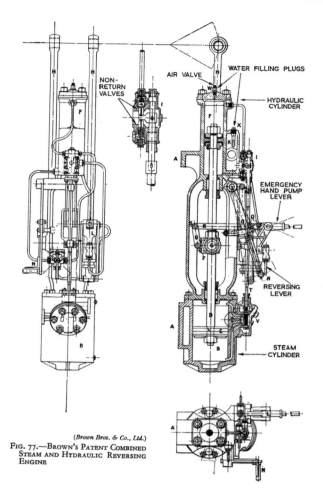

FIG. 77.—BROWN'S PATENT COMBINED STEAM AND HYDRAULIC REVERSING ENGINE

(*Brown Bros. & Co., Ltd.*)

Brown's Steam and Hydraulic Reversing engine. (Author's collection)

The piston rod was in turn connected to a crosshead and a pair of vertical linking rods to a bell-crank on a reversing or Wyper shaft.

On the reversing shaft were mounted four bell-cranks and reversing arms which were connected to the beam drag link pins. A lever connected to the hydraulic cylinder changed the position of the steam piston, thus the two vertical rods were actuated to the Wyper shaft and all the four bell-cranks to the valve gear operated simultaneously. The reversing gear was controlled by a lever on the inboard side of each main engine by the starting platform.

The movement of this reversing linkage could be adjusted to control the required 'cut-off' point that the steam was admitted into the cylinders and thereby control the required degree of steam expansion within the cylinders. At 'full ahead' speeds a cut-off point of 40 per cent to 45 per cent of the piston stroke could well be used. In this manner after the steam was cut-off it expanded until the end of the stroke.

Stuffing Boxes and Glands

On main engine piston rods and slide valve rods and with all other steam-driven auxiliary machinery it was necessary to 'seal' in the steam into the piston area to prevent steam and condensate leakage. The main reason for this was to enable the steam to expand and use its energy effectively and also to prevent the oil in the sump of the main engines from contamination by water.

The sketch below shows a detailed section through a stuffing box and its construction. In the case of the main engine cylinder it had a projected flange cast integral with it. During manufacture this was bored out to a diameter larger than that of the piston rod and formed an annular space into which packing could be inserted. The packing of the correct width was put in separate layers around the rod until the box was nearly full. Each successive layer was cut to the required length (the circumference of the piston rod). The packing piece was bent around the rod and inserted into the box so that the ends of each layer butt together but did not coincide with the preceding one. This helped to prevent the steam leaking past the ends. The gland (plate) was then inserted and made to compress the packing by tightening up the nuts on the studs. This operation should ensure that the nuts were never screwed up tighter than necessary to just prevent steam leakage, or excessive friction between and piston rod would result.

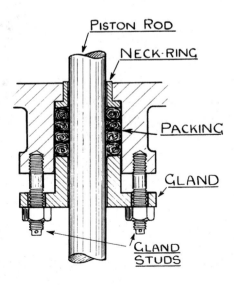

Left: A sketch of a typical stuffing box for a piston rod. Its main function was to maintain steam tightness but at the same time to allow a rod or shaft to move with minimum friction and wear. This was always difficult to achieve. (Author's collection)

Right: The *Britannic's* port main engine finished in works. Under the large steam 'eduction' pipe to top left is the shiny vertical connecting link to the reversing weighshaft of which one of its links are near to camera. (MaritimeQuest)

7

REPUTATIONS, STEREOTYPES AND URBAN MYTHS

Noted maritime historian, John Maxtone-Graham once recorded about the Black Gang that:

> … hideous conditions nurtured a breed of ruthless men. On British ships, they were invariably Liverpool-Irish and on others, the brutal dregs of half a dozen nationalities; whatever the blend violence seemed preordained, often lethal. Drunken stokers, sometimes wheeled in barrows back on board ship, used to embark upon fearful battles, going after each other with slice bars, tongs, shovels, anything that came to hand. Mates [navigators/deck officers] had a standing order when the Black Gang fought: close the hatches and stand clear.

The tough, hard-working image of the fireman was captured by former merchant seaman John Lennox Kerr writing under the pen name Gavin Douglas, in *Seamanship for Passengers*, in which he wrote about the passing of coal-fired ships:

> Oil fuel is rapidly displacing coal even in cargo ships and the old type of fireman with his sweat-rag round his neck and his brawny arms developed by handling shovel and slice bar is following the sailing ship seaman into the past. If we regret the passing of the tough Liverpool-Irisher and the impatient rattle of his shovel on the stokehold plates as he summons the trimmer with more coal, no one will regret the passing of his task. In heavy weather, with water streaming down the ventilators until he worked in a slush of coal dust and water to his ankles and a cold pillar of air chilling his shoulders even as the front of his body was

being roasted by the heat from the opened furnaces, his was no soft toil. The death rate among ships' firemen was very high and there is little to wonder at in this. I have a vivid memory of men in the stokehold of a ship steaming down a hot and airless Red Sea. There was not enough breeze to cool those on the upper deck, and down in the stokehold the heat would have been unbearable for anyone but a ship's fireman. The fires had to be raked and shaken up every few minutes to make them burn. The ship had no artificially 'forced' draught and no 'natural' air came down the wide-mouthed ventilators. The fires burned only by the incessant toil of the coal-blackened blasphemous men whose pride is in keeping up a full head of steam.

These men work a 4-hour watch at the fires. In those 4 hours they must clean out 1 or 2 huge fires yet hold their steam. They come from the stokehold every now and then to lean over the ship's rail and suck in the hot outer air and to drink gallons of tepid water. The water passes through their bodies and the pores of their skin, and they can sweat no longer. At the end of their watch they are sucked of all energy, bleached white under the coal dust by the heat of fires and boilers.

They end their watch by filling 20 to 30 large buckets with ashes and then they come on deck and wash the coal dust and dried sweat from themselves. Six hours later they are called from their bunks to haul up another 20 to 30 buckets of ashes and dump these over the side before going to the stokehold for another 4 hours of Hell.

But they always kept the steam up. There is red line at a certain part of the steam gauge and the fireman's task is to keep the gauge pointer trembling at that red mark. If it falls away from the mark, the engineers are demanding to know why. If it passes the red mark the extra pressure forces open a safety valve and a white plume of steam hisses loudly from a pipe against the after side of the funnel. A fireman so unskilled that he allows the boilers to 'blow off' has committed a professional crime that cannot be hidden. The escaping steam makes a sound that deafens the ears of everyone on board. Now and then, as when a ship has to stop unexpectedly, this 'blowing off' cannot be avoided.

But a good fireman keeps the needle just under the red mark on his gauge. This marks the pressure in pounds per [square] inch required to drive the engines.

This account was probably on a cargo ship on the Far Eastern run; nevertheless it is a chronicle from a former merchant seaman.

Firemen hard at work in the stokehold. To the left the fireman appears to be raking the coals with a firing hoe above his shoulder height, while the one on the right is bending down cleaning the grate with a slice. All under the supervision of the boiler-suited engineer. (Maurizio Eliseo)

The more formidable reputations of firemen preceded them and have been documented with some notorious descriptions by various writers and observers has them down as: 'tough fellows, a proportion of them being coarse, truculent individuals who came and went'; 'most of [*Titanic's*] stokers were illiterate and superstitious, always ready to get drunk between stopovers'.

A more balanced description has them down as: 'The Black Gang were hard-swearing, stout-hearted men of rough exterior, but for the most part good-humoured and friendly, despite their strenuous duties.' Harland & Wolff's formal Technical Director C.C. Pounder wrote in an extract from a technical paper in which he put forward a case against coal as:

On leaving port, many firemen and trimmers would be the worst for liquor; consequently, until they sobered up, difficulty was experienced in steaming the boilers, the engineers themselves having to take to the shovels. Of stokehold fights and struggles many tales have been told. In one fight, in a North Atlantic liner, the senior engineer concerned [a friend of C.C. Pounder], had a complete finger bitten off! The aggregate actual time for lifting the coal being necessarily short, the time rate of expenditure of physical effort was undoubtedly great and beyond the capacity of many men to withstand. Add to this the heat, the discomfort, the rolling of the ship, the ofttimes poor quarters, and it is not remarkable that few men were firemen from choice. In a large passenger ship, running to an exacting schedule, life could be harder than in a cargo carrier.

A contemporaneous quote from Alfred Fanstone, a Southampton resident noted about firemen in general: 'They all came home like walking skeletons, the stokers, and they had one glorious booze up, which led to fighting, and then off they went again.'

By the time the *Olympic* and *Titanic* entered service things were changing with the improved accommodation and conditions of service. White Star engineers and officials who had the duty of signing on firemen for the Atlantic run had learned to overlook the muscle-bound, burley types in favour of men of normal stature, or even smaller, who knew their work. The main attributes looked for were fitness, strength, stamina and endurance and also a high tolerance for heat was mandatory as the temperatures in the stokehold sometimes reached 120°F. They needed the intelligence to pace themselves and the ability to work as a team. The *Titanic*'s firemen who testified at the British Inquiry of the disaster were often articulate and obviously intelligent, yet they were treated as if they were uneducated lower class labourers, an attitude born of the tremendous class distinction of the period.

With nigh on 17,000 men unemployed in Southampton at the time it was a hirer's market. As previously referred to, White Star preferred those from Liverpool-Irish stock because they could deliver the goods, so to speak. Now, by some accounts, Liverpudlians by nature could be fiery-tempered, aggressive, argumentative, belligerent, cantankerous or just plain 'bolshie' and bearing in mind the City of Liverpool was settled by Irishmen from both traditions, both Catholic and Protestant, this could lead to friction, especially with the issue of Home Rule for Ireland high on the political agenda. (Liverpool has in the past been referred to as 'the capital of Ireland'.) Their reputation preceded them and they were renowned for being hard-swearing, hard-drinking and hard-fighting. That said, they were hard-working quick-witted and engendered a spirit of camaraderie. Other causes of friction leading to fighting could well be arguments over

These firemen seem to have plenty of room. Note the shovelling with legs apart, to give stability and to counteract the ship's motion. The white cloud emulating from the boiler on the left is a large flame or 'blowback'; a fireman may just be discerned in its glare. (Underwood & Underwood)

women, crowded living conditions, unclean and unwashed individuals or covert homosexuality among a minority of the Black Gang, although anecdotal evidence of the latter seems non-existent.

Firemen and trimmers were a tough breed and needed careful supervision; only the more senior engineers were likely to have been allocated that task, as dealing with such men required experience and understanding. For engineers on watch, authority alone was not enough but the ability of dealing with the Black Gang came from knowing their ways. In the wake of the *Titanic* disaster it was revealed that great difficulty existed in getting firemen to take part in a boat drill as they didn't regard it as part of their work.

One of the *Titanic*'s firemen, 33-year-old William Mintram, had previously been convicted of the manslaughter of his wife in October 1902. At the time he had been living in Winton Street, St Mary's, in Southampton with their five children. He was jailed for the act. Years later, according to witnesses on the night of the sinking, Mintram was seen giving his life-jacket to a fellow crew member before he went down with the ship. His body was never recovered.

The traditional lore and culture of the stokehold was documented by Charles Lightoller, *Titanic's* surviving second officer, in his biography *Titanic and Other Ships* when upon joining the *Oceanic* (1899) following the *Titanic* Inquiry, he bemoaned the absence of one of the characters from the stokehold, a leading fireman known as Old Ned:

Actually, he was responsible for the stokehold crowd, and a tougher bunch than the firemen on a Western Ocean mail boat it would be impossible to find. Bootle seemed to specialise in the Liverpool Irishman, who was accounted to be the toughest of the tough, and prominent amongst the few that could stand up to the life, where life below consisted of one endless drive. Even the engineers seemed to get tainted with that unqualified 'toughness', for they must be able to hold their own with the worst. This type reached its peak in the days of the old *Majestic* and *Teutonic*. The conditions, under which firemen laboured in these boats, were inhuman. Little blame if the men did become brutes. The heat of the stokehold alone, when driving under the last ounce of steam, was terrible. Added to this, when in the Gulf Stream, was the intense humidity.

It was no uncommon sight to see a man, sometimes two, three or even four in a watch, hoisted up the ash shoot with the bucket chain hooked roughly round under their arm-pits, to be dumped on deck unconscious. A few buckets of water over them and then they were left to recover. Neither must they be long about it, or up comes the leading fireman, who, with strict impartiality, will apply both boot and fist to drive his dogs of war below again.

The instructions were to keep up that 'arrow,' indicating the steam pressure, at all costs regardless of body or bones. Small wonder at the tales that used to creep about of men gone missing after a free fight, when sharp shovels are used as flails.

'So and so missing. He must have gone overboard during the night. Caught with the heat, poor beggar.'

Yes, caught all right, but perhaps with the sharp edge of a shovel.

An engineer at one time was seen to go into the stokehold and never seen to come out, nor yet seen on deck. He was a particularly powerful type of man and brutal withal, who hazed his watch to the limit in the demand for steam till the stokehold was Bedlam let loose. From that day till this – though never mentioned ashore – his disappearance was frankly attributed to the swift cut of a shovel from behind, and his body shot into a furnace. The truth will never be known, but from then on, an engineer never went into the stokehold unaccompanied by his leading hand. [For a human body to be fed into a furnace, the door would have had to be wide or the person a very small engineer.]

Later, Lightoller wrote of his appointment to the *Oceanic*:

With the *Oceanic*'s comfortable quarters, and bathrooms, there was no call for the tough element; in fact it did not exist in Southampton, where the mail boats were now running from.

A sympathetic account from a career White Star officer but not all the hard element had been exorcised from the Merchant Navy's Black Gangs as an account from Henry Clow, possibly a leading fireman with a vessel on the South American run, reminiscing about his life at sea back around 1920 revealed:

Steam was going back about two o'clock in the morning, and I knew which boiler was short of steam. So I knew who to go to when I went into the stokehole. An' this feller was a Chilean. So I went in and started to tell 'im off – 'Get the steam up!' So he'd just been slicin' the fire, that's poking. An' of course the slice was pretty well red hot by the time he drew it out. Then he made for me with a red hot poker. Well, fortunately the poker was too heavy for 'im, it dropped. An' I put my foot on it. An' then I just went straight at 'im mad, had a good pair of fists in those days. So I just put 'im on his back, gave 'im quite a nice Halloween party.

Surviving fireman, John 'Jack' Podesta later recalled about 'a run ashore' during which some of his shipmates 'missed the boat'. Prior to the *Titanic* sailing at Southampton, it was after the 8 a.m. muster, on 10 April which took about an hour. Following this he went ashore again with several other firemen and trimmers for a drink at The Grapes public house in Oxford Street:

Six of us left about 10 minutes to 12 and got well into the docks and towards the vessel. With me and my mates were three brothers named

Slade, Bertram, Tom and Alfred. We were at the top of the main road and a passenger train was approaching us from another part of the docks. I heard the Slades say: 'Oh let the train go by', but a mate [William Nutbeam] and myself crossed over and managed to board the liner. Being a rather long train, by the time it passed the Slades were too late; the gangway was down leaving them behind. (With a trimmer, Mr Penney, who lodged with the Slades.)

In Lawrence Beesley's 1912 book *The Loss of the* SS *Titanic*, the surviving second-class passenger wrote:

Just before the last gangway was withdrawn, a knot of stokers ran along the quay, with their kit slung over their shoulders in bundles, and made for the gangway with the evident intention of joining the ship. But a petty officer guarding the shore end of the gangway firmly refused to allow them on board; they argued, gesticulated, apparently attempting to explain the reasons why they were late, but he remained obdurate and waved them back with a determined hand, the gangway was dragged back amid their protests, putting a summary ending to their determined efforts to join the *Titanic*.

Apparently, the crew's gangway was being lifted and the attendant officer (possibly the Master-at-Arms) refused to allow them to board.

There were also three brothers by the name of Pugh, in a similar last mad dash – one turned back, but Alfred and Percy made it onto the ship.

By contrast, 32-year-old Charles E. Judd, a fireman from Southampton, was previously a fireman on the *Oceanic*, but owing to that ship being laid up at Southampton due to the coal strike, he signed on the *Titanic* instead. He was rescued in Collapsible B.

Lawrence Beesley related on the ship's call at Queenstown on 11 April:

As one of the tenders containing passengers and mails neared the *Titanic*, some of those on board gazed up at the liner towering above them, and saw a stoker's head, black from his work in the stokehold below, peering out at them from the top of one of the enormous funnels – a dummy one for ventilation – that rose many feet above the highest deck. He had climbed up inside for a joke, but to some of those who saw him there the sight was seed for the growth of an 'omen,' which bore fruit in an unknown dread of dangers to come.

The sight of a fireman or trimmer was certainly a rare occurrence for passengers but why this was seen as an 'omen' is not known.

The aftermost dummy funnel was not used for carrying away the products of combustion but served as a shaft for air being drawn into the engine room and the galleys and also as a flue from the galley. Inside it there was a ladder which was accessed from the turbine engine room below and it was not unusual for crewmen to climb to the top of the funnel for some fresh air and maybe a quiet smoke.

Also while at Queenstown, and being attended by the passenger and mail tenders *America* and *Ireland*, a fireman by the name of John Coffey 'jumped ship' by hiding among the mail bags until the tender reached shore. Apparently his home was listed as Queenstown on the signing on articles.

Visitors to the stokehold were rare. Passengers would not entertain the thought and they were not particularly welcome in that environment. For the rare visitor who did foray into the closed community it would only be by invitation of the chief engineer or a White Star official. A custom that grew was for the visitor to have his boots encircled with a chalk ring and was thus said to be 'chalked'. This meant that the person had to forfeit some drink money in lieu of a tip.

In Lieutenant Commander Bates's book, *The Merchant Service* published in 1945, he wrote:

In the stokehold are the firemen. In coal-burning ships they have a job beside which Dante's *Inferno* seems like a river trip at Maidenhead. Stripped to the waist, they are slaves to the pressure gauges; they must keep their fires raked clean and fed with fresh fuel, for no fireman dare commit the heinous sin of letting steam pressure fall in his boilers. Sweat, burns and aching muscles are their daily lot, their only solace is the life-giving air which comes down with rain and spray through the 'Fidley' or grating overhead.

All very forbidding yet somehow poetic and somewhat illusionary. While firemen and trimmers may well have worked 'stripped to the waist', most wore vests or singlets at least. The searing heat and embers jumping from furnaces would cause burns and injury. No fireman could afford to be stood down by sustaining burns by not wearing clothing that protected them. Likewise in the bunkers, trimmers would be covered, even their arms, for falling and scratching themselves against sharp coal could cause cuts and abrasions.

8

THE LOW-PRESSURE (LP) OR EXHAUST TURBINE AND CONDENSERS

Aft of the main reciprocating engine room between bulkheads L and M was the turbine engine room in which was situated the low-pressure or exhaust turbine.

LP Turbine – Technical Particulars

Turbine type:	Parsons direct-coupled, Low-pressure Reaction
Turbine mass:	420 tons
Rotor and Blades mass:	130 tons
Diameter of Rotor drum:	12ft
Length of Rotor drum:	13ft 8in
Length overall of turbine:	32–33ft
No of blade expansions:	6
Blade height (1st expansion):	18in
" " (2nd "):	21½in
" " (3rd "):	25½in
" " (4th "):	25½in
" " (5th "):	25½in
" " (6th "):	25½in
No of Blade rows on Rotor:	42
Speed/ Max speed:	170/190 rev/min

The turbine was built to the Parsons multi-stage reaction design with blade lengths ranging from 18in to 25½in in order that the expanded steam from the main reciprocating engines should expend further energy through the turbine before finally exhausting to the condenser. At full speed exhaust

Often wrongly identified as a watertight door, this is actually a large 'swiss' sluice valve for the *Britannic*. The man alongside gives some idea of its size. The valve was installed horizontally at an inclined angle. (John McMillan)

The *Britannic's* forward lower half of turbine casing. (MaritimeQuest)

steam from the two main reciprocating engines entered the turbine at 9psi absolute (or -5.7psi gauge) and further expanded through the turbine blades until it exited the turbine at 1psi absolute (or -13.7psi gauge). The turbine directly drove the *Titanic's* centre four-bladed, cast manganese bronze propeller. The turbine exhaust outlets evenly split and passed into the tops of the two condensers located outboard and abeam of the turbine via large, rectangular ducting. Mounted between the turbine outlets and the inlets to the condensers were two huge sluice valves that operated in a similar fashion to watertight doors. An electric motor operated these and the gate of the sluice valve was moved horizontally, thus sealing off the turbine from operation completely when not required.

Under normal manoeuvring conditions in and out of port or at 'slow ahead' and steaming astern, the *Titanic's* outer screws were used and the centre screw driven by the LP turbine was by-passed and the ship manoeuvred and steered like a conventional twin-screw vessel. When required, two huge changeover valves of the piston type were activated by a Brown's steam engine which operated a link mechanism. The changeover valves' pistons covered or uncovered a series of circumferential ports to the LP turbine or directly to the condenser. In the upper position the ports were open to the turbine, and in the lower position the steam was admitted to the condenser. Both valve pistons were operated by a rocker arm connected to the crosshead of a Brown's steam and hydraulic engine which actuated both valves simultaneously. The Brown's engine was controlled by a lever on the starting platform close to the main reversing gear.

The *Britannic*'s lower turbine casing, prior to being fitted with its blades. (MaritimeQuest)

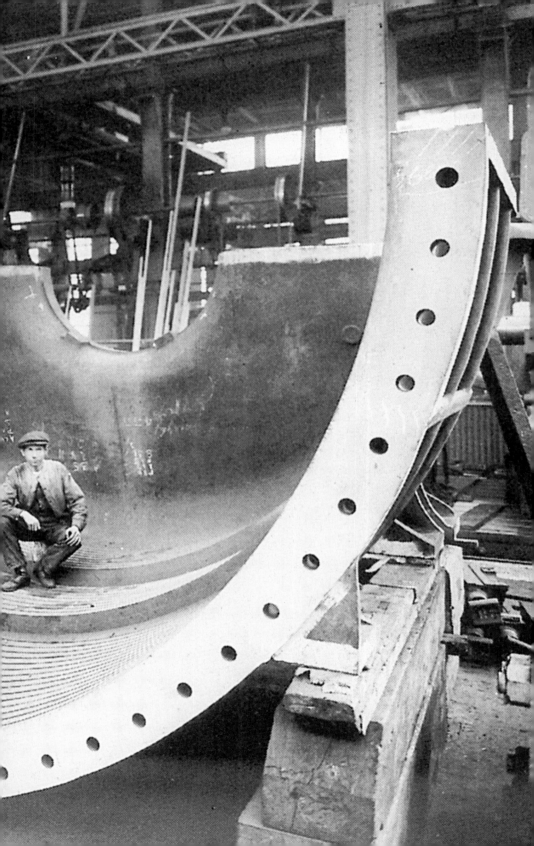

The *Olympic's* turbine rotor being machined in a lathe prior to being bladed. (David Hutchings collection)

When the ship's engines were sufficiently up to speed at 'half ahead' (about 50 rev/min or around 13½ knots), the Brown's engine was operated to activate the valves from by-pass to engage the turbine which gave the *Titanic* an extra 2 knots at 'half ahead' bringing her up to 15½ knots. The turbine speed could be increased proportionately by the amount of steam received from the main engines, up to a maximum of 190 rev/min at full speed.

It is of interest to note that anecdotal evidence from a senior Cunard White Star engineer serving on the 1927-built *Laurentic* with similar combination machinery, later claimed during 1940 that the centre shaft when engaged: 'had no effect on the speed', but 'it took the knocks out of the engines'.

The changeover valves were capable of a form of speed regulation as there was an automatic override whereby the turbine's speed activated a Proell centrifugal governor. This in turn actuated the Brown's engine which operated the changeover valves. If the speed of the turbine rotor exceeded 10 per cent above the maximum number of revolutions set, then the changeover valves would redirect the steam directly to the condensers until the speed of the turbine dropped below the preset desired revolutions. As far as is known there was no braking system on the turbine when not in use.

The *Olympic*'s turbine rotor being fitted with its rows of blades. (David Hutchings collection)

The *Britannic*'s completed turbine rotor being lowered onto trucks in shop. (MaritimeQuest)

One of the inherent problems of the LP turbine was its steam tightness. It was not so much that of steam leaking out but because of its sub atmospheric or partial vacuum condition, it was that of air trying to enter the turbine. In part this was achieved by the seal formed by the butting flange surfaces on the upper and lower casings of the turbine. These were machined ground flat and then finished off by 'hand scraping', a laborious task that could take a week. There was no gasket or sealant used for the mating faces but sometimes a thin film of 'triple-boiled oil' was applied and the casing nuts and studs tightened down. The turbine shafts were 'sealed' at either end of the casing by 'labyrinth' glands which minimised the ingress of air into the turbine. At each end of the casing this consisted of ten circumferential fins on the turbine rotor with ten fins let into the casing. These fins had a radial clearance of about 0.010in ('10 thou'). Outside of these fins were four Ramsbottom-type piston-type rings set into the shaft. The gland was thereby divided into nineteen or so annular spaces which were connected via a pipe and valve to an auxiliary low-pressure steam supply. Sufficient steam was then admitted to produce atmospheric pressure and the existence of this pressure prevented the ingress of air. Often a slight weep of steam into the atmosphere became observable.

The *Olympic*'s completed turbine assembly being installed in the ship's turbine engine room during outfitting. (UF&TM)

The casing of one of the *Olympic*'s changeover valves in the engine works. (UF&TM)

Condensers – Technical Particulars

No of condensers:	2
Length:	20ft
Height:	24ft
Diameter & Material of tubes:	⅞in 60/40 Brass (Muntz metal)
No tubes/condenser:	9,500 approx
Cooling surface/condenser:	25,275ft²

Function

The surface condenser was so called because condensation of the steam took place on the surface of a large number of tubes through which cold seawater was circulated. The condenser was a heat exchanger in which the steam was condensed back to water after doing work in the engines.

The main functions of the condenser were:

- To reduce the back pressure on the main reciprocating units and LP turbine and so enable the engines to develop greater power.
- To enable the steam to be expanded in the main engines' LP cylinders and the LP turbine to a lower pressure than would be possible if the steam was exhausted to the atmosphere.
- To enable the working substance (water) to be used over and over again.

After passing through the LP turbine the steam had expanded down to 1psi absolute (or -13.7psi gauge or 28½in of vacuum), i.e. sub-atmospheric, in the two condensers. The exhausted steam was condensed by coming into contact with the outer surface of the nest of tubes through which seawater was pumped by the seawater circulating pump. A Weir's air pump was also needed to extract the air and condensed water from the bottom of the condenser. Air came into the condenser from the steam, but it could not, like the steam, be condensed, and was therefore removed to maintain a high vacuum in the condenser.

The exhausted steam exited the turbine casing through two large rectangular openings on either side leading to each condenser. As previously mentioned, the steam could also be led directly to the condensers, bypassing the LP turbine, when the main reciprocating engines were running astern or at less than half speed. When the exhausted steam entered the condenser from the top, it was directed downwards, impinging on the manifold of tubes in the main chamber. Simultaneously, cold seawater was circulated through the tubes and heat was removed from the steam and exchanged to the cold tubes causing the water vapour to condense on the tubes in droplets. These would then fall under gravity to the bottom of the condenser chamber. The fresh water collected was then pumped through the return feed system back to the boilers.

Construction

Harland & Wolff's design of condensers were 'pear' or 'heart' shaped in section and not dissimilar to the Weir 'Uniflux' condenser, and the inlet to these ran the full length of the condenser. The 'pear'- or 'heart'-shaped construction was designed such that the steam entering was caused to traverse the cooling surfaces at practically uniform velocity, throughout its passage.

There were no baffle plates or partitions in the body of the condenser so the incoming steam entered and distributed itself over the whole length and breadth of the condenser. As it cooled it shrank in volume and dropped to the bottom of the divergent area of the condenser chamber which

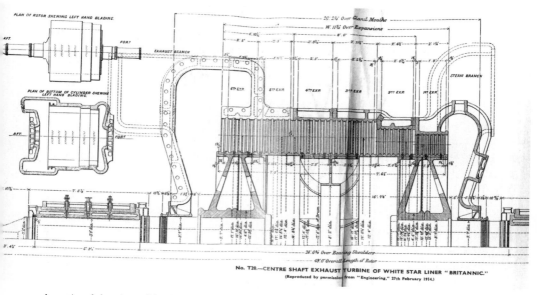

A sectional drawing of the *Britannic*'s exhaust turbine. (Author's collection)

The turbine rotor of the *Britannic* in the process of blading. This turbine was a larger improved modification on those built for the *Olympic* and *Titanic*. (MaritimeQuest)

The *Britannic*'s completed turbine rotor suspended above the lower casing ready for installation. The vertical guide columns are in place to ensure exact location of blading and bearings. The bowler-hatted foreman to the left oversees this delicate task. (UF&TM)

accommodated the smaller volume of the condensate. The construction of the 'pear'-shaped condenser was of a cast-iron chamber flanged at each end to accommodate 1in thick rolled brass tube plates. These plates were drilled with holes ⅞in diameter through which passed some 9,500 Muntz metal tubes per condenser, with a supporting plate in the centre. For each tube, at both ends, small stuffing boxes or ferrules were fitted to prevent the leakage of seawater between plate and tube.

As seawater proved ideal for the condenser cooling, water was drawn from inlets on the underside of the *Titanic*'s hull near the turn of bilge, and circulated through the condensers via two high-volume seawater circulating pumps, and discharged through two outlets just above the waterline. The *Titanic*'s two condensers had a combined cooling surface area of 50,550ft^2. Her auxiliary condenser for ancillary machinery and which was also used in port, was sited on the starboard side of the main engine room; it had a cooling surface of 3,600ft^2.

The low-pressure turbine secured in its position in the *Britannic*'s turbine engine room. The angled locations for the large 'swiss' sluice valves are near the top left-hand corner of the picture. (UF&TM)

The fitting of tubes in the *Britannic*'s starboard condenser. (UF&TM)

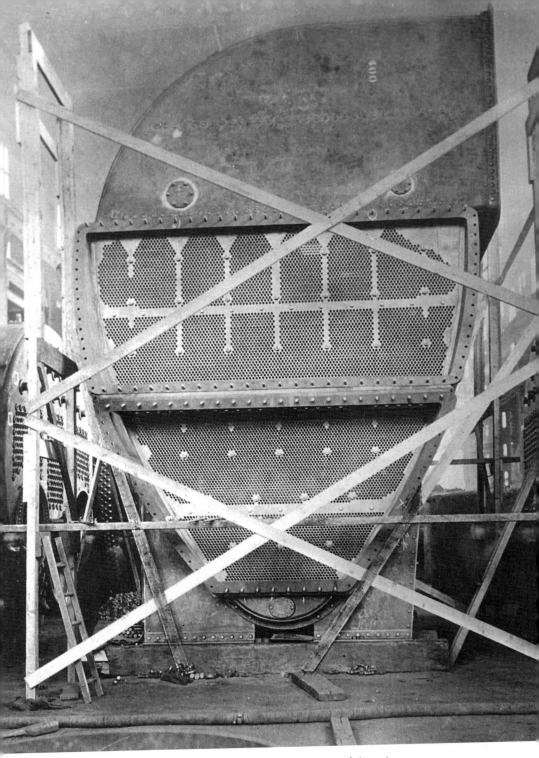

One of the *Olympic*'s main condensers in the boiler shop with its casing
partially removed to show the seawater side nest of tubes. (UF&TM)

Maintenance

Although the condensers contained no moving parts, it was necessary to overhaul the condensers of the 'Olympic'-class regularly to maintain their efficiency. Since it was principally a very large heat exchanger with the heat transfer taking place through the walls of the tubes, it was essential that both the internal and external surfaces of the tubes were kept as clean as possible. The outside (steam side) of the tubes could become coated with a film of oil or grease carried over by steam from the engines. The usual operational procedure to clean this side was to fill the steam side up with fresh water to which was added a good strong solution of soda. Steam would then be piped to the bottom of the condenser and the solution left to boil for several hours, after which it was discharged to the bilges.

On the seawater side the inside of the tubes would in time foul up with a scaly deposit or choke with mud, grit or small shells depending on the waters in which the ship had been steaming. This was drawn in by the circulating pumps when manoeuvring in shallow rivers or ports.

Because of the work involved in removing the large condenser doors this task was generally carried out during drydocking. In which case the blocked tubes would be rodded out with a large wire spiral brush or tube scraper in a similar manner to which the Scotch boiler fire tubes were cleaned.

Leaking or split condenser tubes were usually detected by a rise in the water level or increased density of the boiler water. If it was not convenient to fit new tubes, the defective ones were blanked off by driving in wooden plugs at either end of the offending tube. Later blank-ended ferrules replaced the open-ended ones. While the condenser doors were removed, opportunity was taken to clean their inside surfaces, and coat them with a preservative paint like 'Shellac' or a cement wash.

9

THE BLACK GANG'S STRUGGLE TO SAVE *TITANIC*

The following reports, based on published accounts, of what occurred in the boiler rooms and engine room are as would be expected during an emergency. Some were given at the *Titanic* inquiries and others recalled later in life by letters. All times are approximate and the events not strictly chronological.

At 8 a.m. on Saturday, 14 April 1912 the last of two or three double-ended boilers were flashed up in No 2 boiler room. They were up to working pressure twelve hours later at 8 p.m. and brought on line with the other boilers, thereby increasing the *Titanic*'s speed. At this stage twenty-four out of the ship's twenty-nine boilers were under full steaming conditions.

According to the recollections of Fireman George Kemish:

We were sitting around on buckets-trimmers' iron wheel barrows Etc. I had just sent a trimmer up to call the 12 to 4 watch – it was around 11.25 p.m. 14th April when there was a heavy thud and grinding tearing sound. The telegraph in each section signalled down Stop. We had a full head of steam and were doing about 23 knots. We could have given much more steam pressure had it been required. We had orders to 'box up' all boilers and put on dampers to stop steam rising and lifting safety valves (steam). Well the trimmer came back from calling the 12 to 4 watch and he said 'Blimme we've struck an ice berg'. We thought that a joke because we firmly believed that she had gone aground off the banks of Newfoundland.

Indeed, suddenly the top red panel on the boiler room telegraph illuminated to indicate 'stop'. As boiler dampers were being closed to deal with the intensity of the furnace fires, seconds later at 11.40 p.m., just before the end of the eight to twelve watch, the *Titanic* was in collision with an iceberg. The damage caused was to the bottom of the starboard side of the ship about 10ft above the level of the keel. A breach, thought to be a series of short gashes, extended over a length of 300ft. This breach opened the forepeak, No 1 hold, No 2 hold, No 3 hold, No 6 and No 5 boiler rooms to the sea.

Around 11.41 p.m. all watertight doors were closed from the bridge and Captain Smith ordered 'half ahead' at 11.42 p.m., and at 11.49 p.m. he stopped the ship's engines.

It is for consideration that at this stage bilge pumps were started to deal with the flooding, and also it is a strong possibility that the ash ejection pumps were cross connected in order to pump the bilges. Later, as will be seen, a 10in diameter leather suction hose was brought forward to the flooding boiler rooms. It was connected to a powerful pump in the shaft tunnel that may have been the tunnel well pump that dealt with the ingress of water that lubricated the tail shafts that ran out to the propellers.

In No 6 boiler room where the ship's side plates had opened at the starboard side after end, water immediately poured in some 2ft above the stokehold plates. Initially Leading Fireman Frederick Barrett, Fireman George Beauchamp, from stokehold No 10, together with Junior Assistant Second Engineer Jonathan Shepherd, ran into No 5 boiler room to escape the ingress of water in No 6 boiler room before the watertight door shut. However, they were ordered back to their stations in No 6 boiler room by Second Engineer John Hesketh. They returned by the escape ladder that

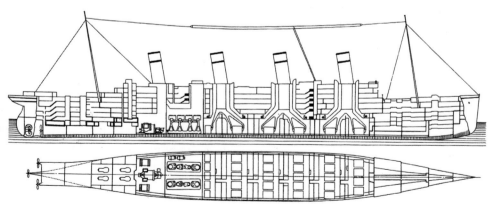

A general arrangement of the *Olympic* showing the boiler and engine rooms and watertight bulkheads. (Author's collection)

led up to E deck and along with other firemen started drawing the fires out until ten minutes after the collision the water was some 8ft above the double bottom and nearly up to the waists of some of the firemen working there. In No 4 boiler room at the time of the collision, Trimmer George Cavell was working in the starboard coal bunker when piles of coal fell on top of him. Not far from him, another fireman was standing stock still, gazing at his bowl of soup which had fallen onto the soot-covered floor from the top of the boiler where he had carefully placed it to warm up ready for consumption when he came off duty at midnight!

At 11.42 p.m. the Black Gang from No 5 boiler room assembled on the Scotland Road (the main working alleyway) and mustered on the starboard side of E deck, but some minutes later at approximately 11.45 p.m. were detailed back to their boiler rooms with the order, 'All hands stand by your stations'.

With all the engines stopped from 'full ahead' there would have been a build up of steam that would exceed the working pressure and cause the safety valves to lift, it was therefore necessary to rake the hot coals or drawing the fires from the boiler furnaces in order to prevent further generation of steam and dampen the coals. To add to the confusion it was no longer possible to cross from one compartment directly to another via the firemen's passage because of the closure of the watertight doors. Instead one had to climb the staircase ladder to above the watertight bulkhead and go down the other side.

At about 11.55 p.m. Second Engineer John Hesketh, in charge of No 5 boiler room, ordered Leading Fireman Charles Hendrickson to bring some lamps. He managed to gather about five and tried to return via the escape ladder to No 6 boiler room. However, upon seeing that it was rapidly flooding, he returned back by the escape ladder to No 5 boiler room and handed out the lamps, after which he returned to his cabin on G deck at around midnight.

No 5 boiler room, although not quite as obvious, was damaged in the starboard forward bunker, about 2ft above the stokehold plates and 2ft from the watertight bulkhead between Nos 5 and 6 boiler rooms. It was estimated that water entered this space at no greater rate than a conventional fire hose! At the time of the collision these bunkers were empty and the bunker door was closed when water was seen entering the ship. At the time there was no indication of damage to No 4 boiler room.

At about 11.52 p.m. it was becoming clear that No 6 boiler room was overwhelmed by the sea, and at 11.55 p.m. the firemen and trimmers in this section were relieved of their duties. Near 11.50 p.m. Chief Engineer Bell gave orders to open the watertight doors forward to the boiler rooms. Trimmer Thomas Patrick Dillon was in the engine room and helped to open the watertight door to No 1 boiler room along with the chief, and then went forward to assist in opening the watertight door to No 2 boiler room.

Meanwhile at around 11.54 p.m. Barrett and Shepherd were relocated in No 5 boiler room where they met up with Junior Assistant Second Engineer Herbert Harvey and Senior Assistant Second Engineer Bertie Wilson attending the pumps, but a phone rang and all the firemen were summoned aft to the engine room with the exception of Barrett. Just after this at about 11.55 p.m., the lights in all six boiler rooms went out at the same time as George Cavell was freeing himself from the piles of coal that had fallen on him in the starboard aft bunker of No 4 boiler room and while he was emerging into the stokehold.

In the adjacent boiler room Barrett was again ordered to proceed aft to the engine room and secure some lamps. Once more he climbed up the escape ladder in No 5 boiler room to E deck where he met a gang of fifteen to twenty firemen, and sent two of them to bring the lamps. Cavell in No 4 boiler room was given the same order and when he reached the port side of E deck or the Scotland Road he encountered a large crowd of steerage passengers heading aft, some were wearing wet clothes but all with lifebelts and luggage in their hands. Quartermaster Alfred Olliver who was liaising between the bridge and the engine room arrived at the door to E deck which led down to the engine room where he saw many firemen, trimmers and greasers who had come up from the stokeholds. Here it seems others had been sent from the boiler rooms to acquire some lamps.

When Barrett climbed back down the ladder into No 5 boiler room with the lamps, the lights had come back on again and nearby boilers were being 'blown down'. Upon his arrival on the plates, Herbert Harvey ordered him to draw the fires (in which the hot coals are raked out onto the plates). Barrett then went back up the escape ladder to E deck yet again to fetch as many firemen as possible to undertake this task. Mustering some twenty men, among whom was George Beauchamp, proved not to be too difficult, as many of them were gathered together near their sleeping quarters. Once back in the boiler room they endeavoured to put out the thirty fires by raking out the hot coals and dousing them down with water. Beauchamp drew the fires in front of coal bunker W where the fire had been.

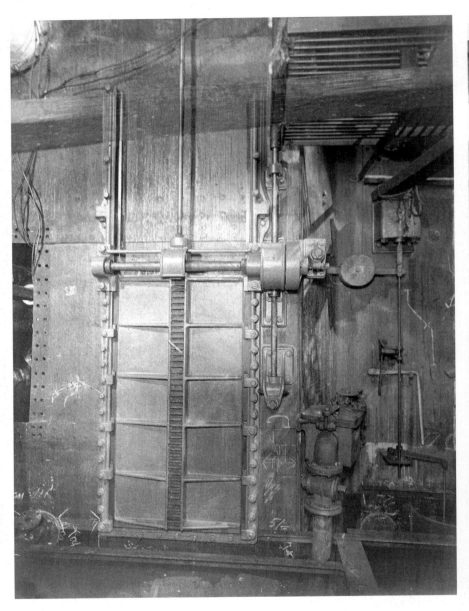

Above: One of the *Olympic*'s watertight doors in the closed position during outfitting.
A daunting sight confronting firemen and trimmers. It could be opened manually from the
forward side by the handle to the right and locating it on the square nut to the mid right of
the door. To open it from aft required prising it open with levers and crow bar! (UF&TM)

Right: The *Olympic*'s watertight door in its open position. To the left is the flange and nuts of
the starboard propeller shaft. (UF&TM)

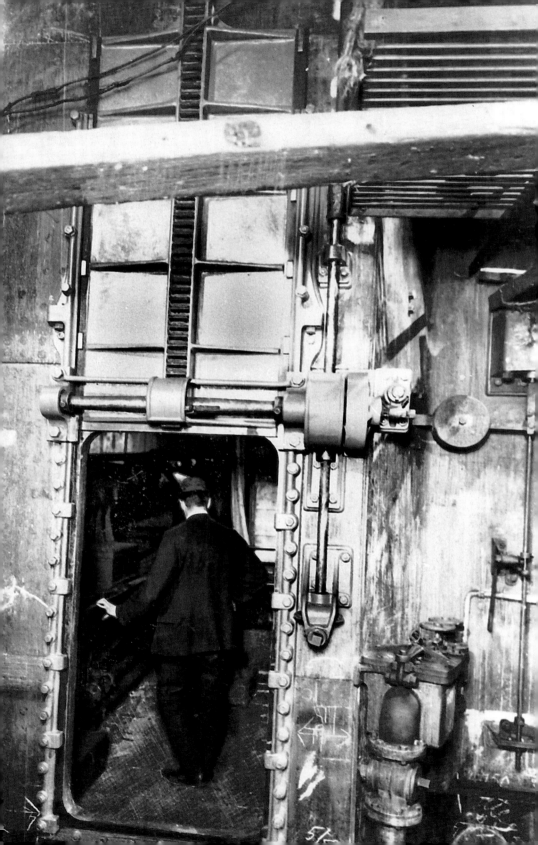

Here the US Navy stokers are raking out or drawing down the hot coals from a furnace, on board the USS *Leviathan* (ex-*Vaterland*). The task for the *Titanic*'s firemen was made even more difficult by rising water and the steam-filled atmosphere. (US Naval Historical Centre/Paul Thompson)

At midnight on the 14 April, Greaser Frederick Scott was stationed in the turbine engine room on the starboard side, just aft of the watertight door leading to the engine room. He wanted to go with a fellow fireman or greaser to free a tunnel greaser locked in the after part of the shaft tunnel. To gain access to the shaft tunnel they climbed up to E deck and walked aft to bulkhead N then down the escape ladder to the forward part of the shaft tunnel. Five minutes later they raised the door to the entrance of the tunnel by 2ft, whereupon the trapped greaser climbed out of the tunnel and the three of them returned to the turbine room at around 12.20 a.m. Simultaneous with this, Greaser Thomas Ranger was detailed off to go to the main switchboard on F deck and shut down all forty-five electric fans and started with the stokehold fans first. When he got there, Ranger started to switch off the stokehold fans beginning with No 6 boiler room. After the shaft tunnel rescue, Scott was ordered to assist in the opening of all the watertight doors and at 12.25 a.m. and helped to open the door at bulkhead M aft of the turbine room.

At 12.20 a.m. on the morning of 15 April, No 5 boiler room fans stop working which caused the combination of hot steam from the coals and the smoke to form smog, which made breathing difficult and visibility poor. Nevertheless by 12.45 a.m. all the boilers' furnaces were free of coal and their doors closed. Following this the majority of No 5's firemen were stood down and sent up from that space. However, Frederick Barrett along with George Kemish and a few others stayed to assist the second engineer in lifting a deck plate on the starboard side so that he could gain access to the valves for the pump. With the poor visibility caused by the smog, Jonathan Shepherd when passing through, failed to see the hole in the plates and fell into it breaking his leg. He was quickly aided by Barrett and Harvey who helped to lift him up and sat him down in the pump room to recover. Following this incident at 1.05 a.m., No 5 boiler room was momentarily dry and all the pumps were working when there was a sudden rush of water surging through the firemen's passage, thought to have been caused by the bulkhead and the bunker wall between Nos 5 and 6 boiler rooms giving way. As previously mentioned, in the first ten minutes it was seen that water was pouring into No 5 boiler room in the forward starboard bunker W, 2ft above the plates. The door to the bunker was shut by Barrett when the water was first discovered just after the collision. This would cause the water to be retained in the bunker until it rose high enough to burst the door which was weaker than the bunker bulkhead; this in effect is what may well have happened. Harvey ordered Barrett to leave, while at the same time Bertie Wilson made towards Harvey to help with Shepherd, and Kemish rushed to the escape ladder. The two engineers were not seen again.

Prior to this at 1 a.m., Greaser Alfred White was in the generator flat and started the emergency generator under the orders of William Parr (Harland & Wolff Guarantee employee) and Chief Electrician Peter Sloan. This he did and the two engineers linked it up on load via the main switchboard.

The efforts to pump and save No 4 boiler room had also been under way. All the watertight doors aft of the main engine room were opened after the collision, and half an hour later all the watertight doors from the engine room through to No 4 boiler room were opened. Patrick Dillon had helped to open all the forward doors but the watertight door to No 5 was not lifted by him because he assumed there was too much water in that compartment. This allowed a 'portable' 10in diameter leather suction pipe to be brought through by four men at 12.40 a.m., and five minutes later Greaser Fred Scott had opened all the watertight doors behind aft of the turbine room to the shaft tunnel in order that the pipe could be connected to the pump suction therein and pumping commenced.

Another scene from *A Night to Remember*, showing firemen and trimmers escaping up the ladder from the flooding boiler room. It was filmed at the Metropolitan Water Board's Cricklewood pumping station. (David Hutchings collection)

At around 1.10 a.m. Dillon and Cavell said that they had seen water rising over the deck plates, and at 1.15 a.m. the atmosphere in No 4 was hot and full of steam as Ranger had shut down the stokehold fans to that section, and by this time the water in the forward part of No 4 was rapidly rising. Trimmer George Cavell and Fireman Frank Dymond were drawing the fires along with others when the water reached their knees before being stood down and released by Junior Second Engineer Norman Harrison and Senior Second Engineer William Farquharson. In the following ten minutes, boiler rooms Nos 4 and 5 were lost to the flooding and the *Titanic* was sinking fast, with this in mind the remaining crew in Nos 2 and 3 were instructed to draw their fires.

Around 1.20 a.m. nearly the entire staff of the engine and turbine rooms was released from their duties. One fireman, Patrick Dillon, went aft through the open watertight door into the main engine room along with other engineers and firemen. He recalled that Farquharson gave the order, 'All hands on deck; put your life-preservers on.' Upon which those below climbed the ladder to E deck. Dillon then split from the main group to go aft to the well deck, while Scott, who came up at the same time, together with thirty to forty firemen, paused on E deck until another fireman came down and instructed them to put on their lifebelts. Ranger went up to the starboard side of B deck where he met a group of twenty or so firemen.

Chief Engineer Bell with a handful of men remained below, still drawing the last fires, but also ensuring enough steam to run the emergency generator, and possibly closed the watertight doors that had been opened.

By 1.40 a.m. Dillon who had been ordered up to the boat deck was convinced that most of the engineers had been evacuated from the engine and boiler rooms, but it was possible that some remained at their posts, as Greaser Alfred White later wrote that he stayed down to the last moment until relieved of his duties and ordered up to the boat deck by Anthony Frost and William Parr (these two men were part of Harland & Wolff's nine-man Guarantee Group). He recalled that Parr and the rest of the engineers were below; he arrived on the boat deck just before the *Titanic* broke in two. At 2.18 a.m. the *Titanic's* lights failed and two minutes later she foundered and claimed the lives of 224 engineers, greasers, firemen and trimmers. As the waters closed over the *Titanic's* stern at 2.20 a.m. that morning the wages for surviving crew members ceased forthwith. In all, the surviving tally from the engine room was three leading firemen, four greasers, forty-four firemen and nineteen trimmers.

10

OTHER LABOUR-INTENSIVE AUXILIARIES TO ATTEND

Feed Water Filters

The condensate from the condensers was drawn off by extraction or air pumps and delivered to two 2,790-gallon feed tanks from which it drained into two 300-gallon hotwell tanks. It was in these tanks that any fresh water was made up from the ship's three evaporators to make up for any leakage in the steam cycle system. From the hotwells the feed water was extracted by two pairs of Weirs hotwell pumps. One pair served each tank and discharged to two pairs of feed water filters. The feed water filters were placed in the feed system to remove any suspended impurities (mainly oil) from the feed water. In a reciprocating engine the pistons and slide valves required constant lubrication. Some of the oil would become entrained in the steam, and, unless removed, would be pumped back into the boiler. This would result in some of the heating surfaces becoming coated, and as a result would cause overheating with a consequent loss of strength (q.v.).

In the *Titanic's* case, the filters were situated between the condensate extraction (air) pumps and the boiler feed pumps, whereby the water flowed through the filters due to the force of gravity. There were four placed against the forward engine room bulkhead. They were supplied by Messrs Railton, Campbell & Crawford and had a total filtering area of 1,008ft².

Operation and Cleaning

Inside the vessel was one filter element made up of twenty-six perforated plates (like a giant version of a cafetière plunger), in between which was placed disc-shaped sheets of felt or 'Terry' towelling to form a super sand-wich. On the filter vessel inlet and outlet valves, a by-pass valve and a pres-sure differential gauge were fitted. Also fitted was a soda cock with steam

The *Titanic*'s main feed filters with their covers and elements removed prior to fitting on board. (*The Shipbuilder*)

inlet, and at the bottom of the filter vessel was a drain cock. The assembled filter element would be horizontally located on a spindle and secured with a nut inside the chamber. A cast-iron cover secured with twenty-four nuts completed the unit.

As the filter element clogged with oil, or particles collected as the feed water passed through the filter, the differential gauge indicated the degree of silt and clogging that occurred. At some predetermined pressure indication, say about 15psi, the filter was isolated by opening the by-pass valve and shutting the inlet and outlet valves. The soda cock having been filled with soda was then opened while the filter was full of water then steam was allowed to boil the element and Terry towelling cloth. Any impurities in the intercepting material would be freed to fall to the bottom of the vessel. The drain cock was opened to allow any silt or sludge and the water to drain out. Any resulting drain cock blockage had to be cleared. Following this the whole filter assembly was blown through with steam before putting the filter back on stream.

When the filter differential pressure rose to about 25psi above the usual pressure, the towelling cloth or felt were cleaned or changed. One diagnostic feature was if an engineer had observed that the pressure had risen to its limit and decided to renew the filter cloths. Then having acquired the necessary tools and upon his return found that the pressure had fallen to the usual pressure as with clean elements. This was a good indication that the cloths had become so dirty that they had ruptured, thereby reducing the differential pressure and requiring new elements to be fitted. The filter vessel would be isolated and drained down via the drain cock. Once the vessel was empty its twenty-four nuts of the cover were undone with a spanner and the cover supported by an eye-bolt and chain pulley then swung away. The filter element was then removed from its centre spindle and all cloths renewed.

Thrust Collars and Block

The action of a ship powering through the water is affected by the reaction of the screw(s) against a horizontal column of water which is pushed astern away from the vessel. This resulted in an equal push forward against the propeller shaft, amounting in large ships to some hundreds of tons. If this thrust was not harnessed in some way it would try to push the engine crankshaft, and the connecting rods and piston rods would be forced out of line and strained by the forward movement caused by the thrust of the propeller. The thrust block and its collars were installed to prevent this tendency and were the arrangement whereby the thrust of a propeller was applied to the ship to propel it along.

For a ship the size of the *Titanic's* horsepower, coupled aft of each main engine was the thrust shaft 2ft 3in in diameter with a 9in bore through it. This revolving shaft consisted of fourteen collars, arranged seven at each end, supported at each end and in the middle by journal bearings. These collars would have been produced by turning them from a larger diameter shaft of forged steel with coupling flanges at either end. The thrust shaft was located in the thrust block, a long cast-iron hollow box shape, rectangular in plan.

The inner bottom of the block was formed so that it held a considerable quantity of oil into which the collars on the shaft dipped. The cast-iron thrust block was in turn firmly bolted down to its seating by bolts through the bottom flanges, the seating was itself riveted to the tank top. To relieve the holding down bolts of the shearing stresses encountered, angle iron bar chocks butting against the forward and after end of the thrust block were riveted to the seating. At each end of the block and in the middle was a bearing lined with white metal in which the shaft journals ran.

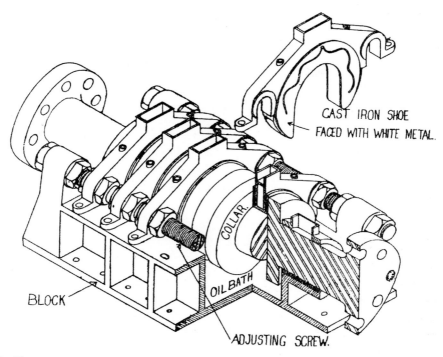

CAST IRON SHOE
FACED WITH WHITE METAL.

COLLAR.

BLOCK

OIL BATH

ADJUSTING SCREW.

An illustration of a thrust block assembly showing thrust collars and 'horseshoe' pads.
The 'Olympic'-class had fourteen collars each. (Author's collection)

Two stationary heavy rods of Muntz metal of 2in or 3in diameter
threaded their entire length were fitted one on either side of the block and
secured into cast bosses at each end of the block. These rods were parallel to the thrust shaft and each assembled with a total of thirty-four brass
adjusting nuts.

The collars on the thrust shaft rotated against cast-iron thrust 'shoes'.
These were fitted into the spaces between the collars and occupied the full
width of the thrust block. There were sixteen thrust shoes made from cast
iron in 'U' form shaped like a horseshoe, and faced on both flat sides with
white metal and had a thrust area of $3,430in^2$ per engine. The thrust shoes
had lugs which projected over the sides of the block and engaged on the
threaded rods, with adjusting nuts on both sides of each lug to maintain
the shoes in their correct position. Minor adjustment of the shoes in a fore
and aft line was controlled by these nuts.

The collars on the thrust shaft transmitted the propeller thrust to the
thrust shoes, which in turn transmitted it to the thrust block and then
to the hull of the ship. No thrust was actually transmitted to the engine's

The *Britannic*'s set of completed thrust blocks. (UF&TM)

crankshaft, and the thrust shoes had initially been adjusted during construction such that there was a minimum running clearance between the crank webs and the ends of the main bearings. Ahead thrust was taken up between the forward side of the collars and the after faces of the thrust shoes, the forward face of the shoe taking the thrust when the engine was running astern. The shoes were cast hollow and seawater was circulated through them to prevent overheating of the running surfaces due to friction and any possibility of the white metal melting or 'wiping'.

Generally each side of the horseshoe had a white metal plate with oil grooves attached to the shoe by dowels and recessed cheese-headed bolts so that they could be removed if necessary and a packing 'shim' inserted behind it to take up any wear. The forward side of the shoe wore very little and required no more than careful attention. The lower portions of the collars ran in an oil bath while the horseshoe white metal faces were supplied by oil from wick lubricators at their tops.

With regard to the LP exhaust turbine, this had an enclosed thrust block forward with sixteen collars of 2ft 8in diameter on a 2ft shaft. The shaft

Above: One of the Harland & Wolff's designed double-cylinder watertight door as fitted aboard the 'Olympic'-class. (*The Shipbuilder*)

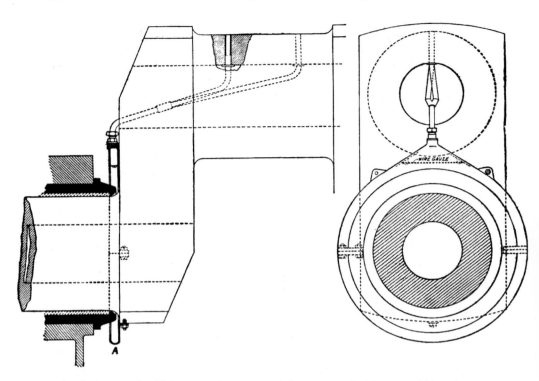

A detail of a centrifugal lubricator. The main crank bearings on the *Titanic* would have been lubricated in a similar fashion. (Author's collection)

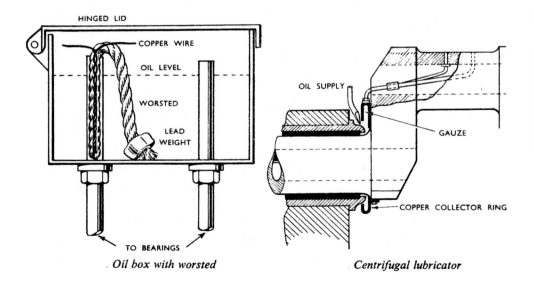

Oil box with worsted   *Centrifugal lubricator*

An oil box with a 'worsted' that performed in the same way as a lamp wick. (Author's collection)

was 4ft 6in long and installed with seventeen thrust shoes with a total thrust area of 5,000in^2.

Watertight Doors

In the *Titanic* the watertight subdivision was designed such that if any two watertight compartments were flooded it would not compromise the safety of the ship. There were fifteen transverse watertight bulkheads which extended from the double bottom to the upper deck at her forward end, and up as far as the saloon deck at her after end. Both extended far above the water line.

The largest compartment was the engine room at 69ft long and aft of this was the turbine room, 54ft long. Boiler rooms were mainly 57ft long with the exception of the one adjacent to the engine room which was 50ft long. Watertight integrity was maintained by eleven watertight doors of the 'drop' type designed by Harland & Wolff which closed vertically downwards when activated.

Doors could be opened and shut manually by a simple cranking handle which operated a helical gear which turned the 'worm' on the end of a shaft that engaged with a 'worm wheel'. This then turned a horizontal shaft with a gear pinion in its middle that meshed with a vertical rack integral with the door.

The doors were normally kept open for access to the firemen and trimmers during the watch changeover. In the event of an emergency all doors could be operated from the bridge. By the flick of a switch the officer of the watch could activate the closing of the doors. Each door was held open by a friction clutch sensitively counterbalanced such that a powerful electro-magnet whose solenoid was integral with a rod that could pivot and release it. When activated the rod and counterbalance disengaged a pawl and ratchet mechanism that allowed the door to close slowly under its own weight. As a further precaution floats were installed beneath the floor plates, and in the event of water entering the compartments, would automatically lift and close the doors of the said compartments if they had not already been closed.

A ladder or escape was provided in each engine and boiler room and other compartments such that the closing of the watertight doors at any time did not seal the personnel working therein. Electric alarm bells near each door rang prior to each door closing.

Four 400kW engines and dynamos generated the power for the lighting and power for the entire ship. They were located abaft the turbine engine room at the after end of the ship. Here is the *Olympic*'s port main generator set on board. (UF&TM)

Lubrication

The remit to keep moving and rotating parts well lubricated and greased fell to the greasers.

In slow-running machinery like the steam reciprocating engines of the *Titanic*, where the speed of rotation was often not more than 75 rev/min, frictional heat was generated at the bearings by reason of heavy pressures acting with low rubbing speeds. With a good lubricant like a mineral oil, the temperature rise necessary to enable radiation and conduction to proceed as fast as heat was generated was moderate, since there were neighbouring masses of chunky machinery with large exposed surfaces to assist in the rapid dissipation of heat. Once thermal equilibrium had been established a bearing was maintained at an approximately constant running temperature. This may have been so high that the hand could not be held on the bearings for more than an instant, yet, if it was the running temperature for that bearing it would not rise higher unless complications occurred. (One of the anecdotal yarns that has grown up over the years

The *Olympic*'s starboard main generator set in the electric engine room. (UF&TM)

among engineers concerning the correct running temperature of bearings was the advice: 'Spit on the bearing if it spits back it's too hot'.)

Overheating was not always caused by the working load; bad alignment was also responsible for forces of greater magnitude. If the friction was abnormally great, due to the entrance of grit, insufficient lubrication, or poor bearing metal, the temperature increased so much that before the balance of heat flow had been maintained or restored, seizure had occurred or the lining of the bearing melted ('wiped').

Information concerning lubrication of the *Titanic*'s main engines is somewhat scant therefore it was necessary to draw upon what contemporaneous information that was available at the time.

Her engines were of the 'open' construction type whereby the crossheads, connecting rods, valve rods, crankshafts and bearings were exposed and not enclosed in an oil-tight casing. The 'open' type engines were lubricated from oil boxes mounted high on the side of the cylinders with lubricating pipes leading down to the various bearings. The flow was controlled either by 'drip feed' or 'automatic drip feed' devices. For the main pistons the water in the steam gave some measure of lubrication.

Drip feed oil boxes had a series of pipes leading down from each box. The pipes in the box extended above the oil level and were fed by strands of worsted, a wick-like material, one end of which was inserted in the tube, the other end being located in the oil by a small lead weight. The oil soaked along the worsted and dripped down the tube, eventually reaching the bearing concerned. The amount of oil supplied to each bearing was determined by the number of strands in each worsted; however, too many strands wedged the worsted in the pipe and prevented the flow. The worsteds were not inserted until the engines were required, and removed when the engines were shut down, which prevented the oil being siphoned to waste.

On top of the main bearings were situated oil cups which had to be regularly replenished by long-nosed oil cans.

The large end bearings could well have been lubricated through holes in the crank pin journal which were supplied by a forked pipe led through the hollow crank pin from a circular ring of 'U' section which was known as a centrifugal lubricator. The fitting was secured to the side of a crank web and into it oil from the lubrication pipe dripped. The oil was forced centrifugally through the oil pipe in the crank pin and onto the bearing.

The eccentrics of the main engines were similarly fitted with centrifugal lubricators, and the system was also extended to items of auxiliary engines, which had to work for long periods.

In addition to the normal lubrication supplied through oil pipes to the eccentric sheaves and straps, semi-circular baths were often supplied and secured across the engine bed plate. The baths contained a mixture of oil and water into which the eccentrics dipped, the adhering emulsion then lubricated and cooled these components. The bath was generally replenished by the oil and water draining down the rods from the glands and oil boxes. A small drain cock was fitted so that surplus oil and water could be drawn off to prevent splashing.

The *Titanic* carried some thirty-three greasers which meant eleven per watch. It was their duty to maintain all oil boxes to the maximum level with oil, and ensure other oil reservoirs were topped up and that worsteds were primed at all times and not dried out.

Generators

Immediately aft of the LP exhaust turbine room and located each side of the centre shaft driven by the turbine, were four sets of steam driven electric generators which supplied power and lighting to the *Titanic*. These were enclosed steam reciprocating engines with their own integral forced lubrication system. Each generator had one high-pressure cylinder of 17in bore and two low-pressure cylinders of 20in bore; all with a combined stroke of 13in. Steam was supplied at 185psi and at maximum speed of 325 rev/min could produce 580ihp. Exhaust from these was routed either via a service heater or to the auxiliary condenser. The reciprocating prime-movers were directly coupled to a compound wound, continuous current dynamo manufactured by W.H. Allen of Bedford. They produced an output of 4,000A at 100V (400kW), with a total output power of 1600kW.

In addition to the four main generating sets there were two 30kW auxiliary generators located in a recess off the turbine engine room at saloon deck level, well above the waterline. They were of compound expansion with a 9in bore high-pressure cylinder and 12in bore low-pressure cylinder with a combined stroke of 5in, and ran at 380 rev/min. The auxiliary generator sets were connected by means of a separate steam pipe cross

The main control platform of a large twin-screw steamship. To the left are the manoeuvring levers on each engine, comprising the levers for cylinder drains, the Brown's reversing engine and the throttle or regulator. On the right the large hand wheels to control the main steam stop valves to the engines. (Author's collection)

connected to boilers situated in several boiler rooms, and in this way the auxiliary generators were available for emergency use should the main sets be out of action.

During the *Titanic's* sinking, by virtue of their position in the ship, the main generators were not initially affected by the flooding provided that the boiler rooms which were flooded could keep them supplied with steam.

Aspects of Main Engine Operation

Prior to starting the main engines all the boilers would be raised to full steam and all boiler main steam stop valves opened to the common supply steam main. The engine room bulkhead main steam stop valves would be open and steam made available up to the main regulating valve (or throttle). Oil pipes were proved clear by oil from a hand feeder. The links, link blocks, bell-cranks, Wyper shaft and drag links were oiled and run over to full travel in both directions by the hand reversing gear after which Brown's reversing gear was engaged. The cylinders were warmed through and heated by careful admission of steam through the valves by easing the regulating valve.

Drain cocks or valves, which were fitted to the top and bottom of each cylinder to remove the water of condensation from each end of the cylinder were operated from the starting platform, were opened. The drains led to the auxiliary condenser.

When manoeuvring the engines the watchkeeping engineers would be at the centre of the bottommost platform called the starting platform. This was located between the two main engines adjacent to the forward LP cylinder columns. The main levers for engine operation were the direction lever which operated the Brown's reversing engine, the regulating lever, the change over valve operating lever and an adjacent panel of levers that controlled the drain cocks.

When entering or leaving port the *Titanic's* chief engineer, along with two senior engineers and three junior engineers, would take up station on the starting platform. The chief engineer's function was to oversee the safe, smooth and efficient operation of the engine room machinery while manoeuvring of the vessel was in progress.

When the order came from the bridge via the engine room telegraph ringing (the first order prior to sailing was always 'stand by'), a junior engineer on each would answer the telegraph by moving a handle to the requisite movement. Each movement was diligently recorded by the third junior engineer present in the 'movements book', in this was noted each telegraph order and its time on the engine room clock. The two senior engineers operated the control levers on the starting platform, firstly by pulling over the direction lever for ahead or astern which actuated the Brown's reversing engine. The regulating valve lever was then operated which allowed steam to enter the HP cylinder and piston valve, this was eased gently at first to turn over the engine and control the steam through the cylinders, and gradually pushed forward to speed up the engine. When manoeuvring was finished and the engines were under 'full away', the cylinder drain valves were shut after all the condensate had been blown out.

When coming toward the end of passage and alongside or at anchor when the engines were no longer required, the last telegraph order was 'stop'. As there was no 'finished with engines' order on the telegraphs this instruction was given verbally by the officer of the watch down the voice pipe to the manoeuvring platform.

11

AFTERMATH AND REPERCUSSIONS

Surviving members of the crew, among them four greasers, forty-four firemen and nineteen trimmers, after they had arrived at New York aboard the rescue ship *Carpathia* were later repatriated in Red Star Line's *Lapland*. Of the arrival in New York to the voyage on the *Lapland*, George Kemish later recalled:

> Us members of the *Titanic* crew were escorted to Wright's Seamens' Mission in West St. were measured up – got two suits of clothes – two pairs of boots, two shirts two suits of underwear. Ties socks etc. Gee I looked a typical Yank when I got home. We came home in the Red Star Line ship *Lapland*. We were landed at Plymouth. All kinds of Officials took our depositions for the Board of Trade Inquiry in London. We were to remain in Southampton while the inquiry was on, to receive five shillings a day, if called to London another 3/6 per day. I was home for three months and then went to sea again. All we got out of it was – what would have been the normal trip's pay – 23 days, our money was then only £5 per month. Our Seamens' Union gave us £3 for loss of Kit. A 'promise' from the White Star Line of a job for life. I have never had anything from them.

George Kemish, like so many of the other seamen who survived, returned to sea and continued serving on ships throughout his working life.

A surviving trimmer, 21-year-old Eustace Philip Snow, was off duty on the night of the disaster, helping to lower one of the lifeboats before making his escape in another boat after the order, 'Every man for himself!' had been issued. After the rescue and his return to Southampton he lived

Red Star Line's *Lapland*, on which the 167 crew survivors, including forty-seven firemen, nineteen trimmers and four greasers, returned to Plymouth. (World Ship Photo Library)

with his parents and shut himself away in his room every 15 April, the anniversary of the sinking. In the local area he earned himself a reputation as being 'a bit of a recluse' and didn't marry until he was 65 years old.

Fireman Jack Podesta recalled:

We came off (duty) at 8 p.m. and went to the galley for our supper. Some of us passed remarks about the persisting cold, so my mate and I put on our 'going ashore coats' and went to the mess room which was up a flight of stairs …

Of the collision he later wrote: 'So, the crash came, it sounded like tearing a strip off a piece of calico, nothing more, only a quiver.'

He was ordered to don his lifejacket and report to one of the lifeboats, but on his arrival he found the craft full and so helped to lower it into the water. Another lifeboat was discovered and Jack was ordered to jump in and steady it as the boat descended down the side of the *Titanic*. He recounted:

I should imagine we were about 500 to 600 yards away from the ship, watching her settling down – she was going down at the head all the time. But there was once when she seemed to hang in the same place for a long time, so naturally we thought the watertight doors would hold her. Then all of a sudden, she swerved and her bow went under, her stern rose up in the air. Out went her lights and the rumbling noise was terrible. It must have been her boilers and engines as well as her bulkheads, all giving way. She then disappeared altogether.

When Jack eventually arrived back in Southampton, the seafarers received their pay, £3 for single men, and £5 for married men.

The *Lapland* sailed from New York on 20 April with 167 surviving crew members, who had not been detained in New York for the US Inquiry, aboard. They were messed in third-class accommodation to protect them from prying journalists but their ordeal was not yet quite over for a bizarre state of affairs awaited their arrival in the UK.

On the 28 April the *Lapland* arrived off Plymouth and anchored in Cawsand bay at 8 a.m. She was attended by three GWR tenders, the *Sir Walter Raleigh* and *Sir Francis Drake* moored both sides aft to disembark the 162 fare-paying passengers and the 1,927 sacks of mail that had been scheduled to be carried by the *Titanic*. The *Sir Richard Grenville* moored forward to take off the surviving crew members and passengers. Prior to this however, White Star officials came aboard and informed the survivors that they would not be allowed off until every one of them had made a deposition. Representatives of the British Seafarers' Union, Messrs Thomas Lewis, the president and A.H. Cannon the secretary, were denied access to the docks or even an invite to sail with a tender, but had chartered a boat and used a loud hailer to alert its members. Lewis, then urged the crew to make no statements without advice, as they embarked on to the tender to take them ashore. The *Titanic's* crew members refused to co-operate with the authorities but after some persuasion, Lewis and Cannon were allowed aboard the tender to meet their members and resolve any impasse and the tender left at midday. Upon their arrival at Millbay Docks they disembarked from the *Sir Richard Grenville* and were billeted in a third-class waiting room until the time-consuming process of collecting witness statements by Board of Trade officials for the British Inquiry was completed; from this some two dozen were summoned to appear before it in London. Also statements were obtained for the White Star Line by Plymouth solicitor, Mr Wilkerson. Food and bedding for overnight accommodation were brought in to the building and a crowd gathered outside. As they were processed one by one they talked to the throng that had assembled through the closed dock gates, minded by the local

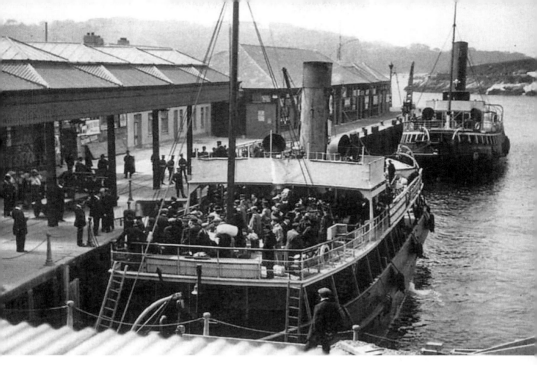

The *Sir Richard Grenville* tender arriving alongside Millbay Dock, Plymouth, with the *Titanic's* crew survivors aboard. (Southampton City Museums)

constabulary. By all accounts it seems that the more militant union members, comprising firemen and trimmers, may possibly have been processed first with the remaining stewards and stewardesses and other clerical staff who were obliged to stay overnight. By 6 p.m. that evening around eight-five of the held crew had been interviewed and 'released' in time to catch a special train for Southampton. The remaining half of the crew returned to Southampton the following day from Plymouth at 4 p.m.

It was reported locally that the Board of Trade, through the Receiver of Wrecks, distributed £50 10s in Plymouth, this was 6s 6d or 7s 6d depending on grade. Mr J. Hanson, District Secretary of the National Sailors' & Firemen's Union, awarded shipwreck pay of £3 to single survivors and £5 to those who were married. In addition there was also a cheque for £300 distribution, from an American benefactor which was to be divided among surviving crew members. It is not known where this was distributed.

While the *Lapland* was steaming across the North Atlantic to Plymouth another drama was being played out on 24 April at Southampton. In accordance with an edict issued by Bruce Ismay, some forty-four extra 'Berthon' collapsible lifeboats, culled from troopships in the port, had previously been shipped aboard the *Olympic* which was due to sail at noon on that day with 1,400 passengers. The ship was under the command of

The replica plaque adjacent to the monument to the *Titanic*'s stewards, sailors and firemen on a fountain in Southampton's Holy Rood Church. (David L. Williams)

Captain Haddock and just as she was about to sail at 11.40 a.m. the entire engine room complement of some 276 firemen, greasers and trimmers, with the exception of three colleagues, ceased work, collected their kits and left the *Olympic*. The remaining staff comprised a storekeeper, an electrical greaser and a refrigeration greaser.

Their discontent had started the previous day with concerns that the forty-four collapsibles were unseaworthy. They sent a request to White Star Line's Southampton Manager, Mr Curry that the collapsibles should be replaced by wooden lifeboats. He tried to reassure them that the boats had been passed by a BoT inspector, but feelings were running high and the Black Gang refused to re-join the *Olympic*. Mr Curry pointed out that the crew's refusal to sail (as they were actually on articles) was tantamount to mutiny under the Merchant Shipping Act of 1894 and that Captain Haddock had every right to order the police to place deserting firemen aboard the ship.

Mr Cannon, Secretary of the British Seafarers' Union, stated that the firemen had left the *Olympic* because the White Star Line would not take proper precautions to save the lives of those aboard the vessel. One of the major concerns was that when the firemen were mustered that morning they found many of the boats, being six to ten years old, to be in a rotten condition; it was even alleged that one man had put his hand through the canvas side of one boat, also when the men tried to open them they could not do so. One of *Olympic's* leading firemen was reported to have said:

What we demand is that every one of the lifeboats shall be a wooden one. Personally, I do not care, as I am unmarried, but many of the men have wives and families, and their lives are as valuable as those of the first class passengers.

Notwithstanding the walk off, all available engine room hands on other White Star and International Mercantile Marine liners in Southampton were seconded to the *Olympic* such that she was able to raise steam and depart just before 2 p.m. that day. She sailed down Southampton Water and anchored off Ryde, Isle of Wight. The following day, 25 April, the *Olympic* proved to be a local crowd-puller with dozens of small craft and excursion vessels with sightseers sailing around the liner.

There was a move by seventy-two first-class passengers to volunteer as firemen and trimmers but this was declined by the master, as the company had hastily recruited 100 men locally in Portsmouth and 150 more by special train from Liverpool and Sheffield. However, when these men eventually reached the *Olympic* by tug that night, the seamen aboard vehemently objected to the strike-breakers joining the ship, on the grounds that were non-union members and unqualified to carry out the work. Many seamen started to leave the *Olympic* and board the same tug and Captain Haddock urged them to return, without effect. When the tug returned to Southampton the following morning fifty-four seamen were arrested and brought before magistrates on 30 April on a charge of mutiny, which was adjourned until 4 May. On 26 April the *Olympic* aborted the scheduled sailing and returned to Southampton that evening where the passengers disembarked for other ships at around 8 p.m. The *Olympic's* sailing was delayed until 15 May, the passengers' fares having been refunded. Ironically in London on the same day (26 April) an official of the National Sailors' & Firemen's Union said of the breakaway British Seafarers' Union's stance: 'We are afraid that the men have been badly advised and regret their action because it will leave a bad impression and bring firemen generally into disrepute.'

As a footnote to this incident, the fifty-four seamen accused of mutiny appeared before Portsmouth Magistrates on 4 May. Although guilt of mutiny was proven, no fines or imprisonment was meted out. It seemed that, following the *Titanic* disaster, public opinion had swung against White

Star and that sympathy lay with the strikers for punishment or fines over concerns about safety would be expedient.

One of the most incredulous stories that came to light in later years was that of 24-year-old Fireman Arthur John Priest from Southampton. He had worked his entire merchant navy career as one of the Black Gang and he was lucky enough to sign on the *Titanic* as he had previously served on the *Olympic*. In fact, he was on board *Olympic*'s fifth voyage from Southampton on 20 September 1911 when she collided with the warship HMS *Hawke* in The Solent that day. When the *Titanic* struck the iceberg Priest was off duty, resting between watches. The route to the deck along with fellow trimmers and firemen took him up through the maze of gangways and corridors before they all reached the deck, but by the time they emerged into the bitterly cold night air most of the lifeboats had already gone. Along with the others Priest swam through the icy waters and was eventually picked up by a lifeboat, and later suffered from frostbite.

In the First World War Priest was serving on board the Armed Merchant Cruiser *Alcantara* when she encountered the German surface raider *Greif*, disguised as a Norwegian vessel, at the entrance to the Skagerrak on 29 February 1916. As the *Alcantara* approached, the *Greif* opened fire. There then followed a short, ferocious, close-range battle, at the end of which both ships were sunk. Some sixty-eight of Priest's shipmates were killed and he only narrowly escaped with shrapnel wounds.

When he returned to work he joined White Star's third 'Olympic'-class liner, the *Britannic*. On her sixth round voyage on 21 November 1916 she struck a mine off Port St Nikolo in the Kea Channel and sunk with the loss of twenty-one lives. Following his survival from *Britannic*, he managed to survive yet another sinking! On 17 April 1917, he was a fireman aboard the Irish Sea ferry *Donegal*, which was serving as a hospital ship when it was torpedoed and sunk in the English Channel. He suffered a head injury and did not serve again during the First World War. He claimed later in life that men refused to sail with him because he brought bad luck! Notwithstanding his good fortune at surviving all the foundering, he died ashore in 1937 aged 49.

Another was 39-year-old Fireman William Clark from Liverpool who also survived the *Titanic*'s sinking. Two years later, on 30 May 1914, he was a fireman aboard Canadian Pacific's *Empress of Ireland* when she sank in dense fog in the St Lawrence River after a collision with the Norwegian steamer *Storstad*, with a loss of 1,014 lives. He survived and in later years recalled:

I was fireman on both the ships. It was my luck to be on duty at the time of both accidents. The *Titanic* disaster was much the worst of the two. I mean it was much the most awful. The waiting was the terrible thing. There was no waiting with the *Empress of Ireland*. You just saw what you had to do and did it. The *Titanic* went down straight like a baby goes to sleep. The *Empress* rolled over like a hog in a ditch.

With only seventy of the *Titanic's* Black Gang and greasers surviving the sinking, small wonder that some of them did not return to sea, although many of them did and it is at this point that their particular story ends.

A contemporary poem published in 1912 summed up the mood and pathos:

Down below in the world of steam
In the heat and fiery glow
Worked hundreds of devoted men
To make the great ship go.

Yet they had wives and children who
Would never see them more
Thinking them safe on the largest ship
That ever left the shore

In Southampton, good old sea port
Wives made widows. What a list
But so recently together
Husbands now forever missed.
(Edwin Drew)

On 22 April 1914 the memorial to the engineers was unveiled by Sir Archibald Denny at the corner of East Park in Southampton and was originally known as the 'Angel of East Park' but latterly as 'The Titanic Memorial'. It was estimated that 100,000 people attended the ceremony. A more modest monument to *Titanic's* firemen in the form of a drinking fountain was also dedicated on The Common at Southampton and unveiled on 27 July 1915 by Mr Bullions Moody. Due to vandalism, this was later moved during 1972 into the shell of Holy Rood Church after its destruction in the Second World War.

12

THE COMING OF OIL-FIRING BUT COAL BURNERS STEAM ON AND ON

Firemen and their RN stoker counterparts played a vital role in the First World War. In fact, following the Battle of Jutland in 1916, Admiral Jellicoe's dispatch was unstinting in its reference to the engineering departments of the fleet under his command:

> Great credit is due to the engine room departments for the manner in which they, as always, responded to the call. The whole fleet maintained a speed in excess of the trial speeds of some of the older vessels … During action the officers and men of that department perform their most important duties without the incentive which knowledge of the course of the action gives to those on deck. The qualities of discipline and endurance are strained to the utmost under those conditions and they were, as always, most fully maintained throughout the operations under review. Several ships attained speeds that had never before been reached, thus showing very clearly their high state of steaming efficiency. Failures in material were conspicuous by their absence, and several instances are reported of magnificent work on the part of the engine room departments of the injured ships. The artisan ratings also carried out much valuable work during and after the action; they could not have done better.
> [In other words: 'Well done stokers!']

From September 1915 the *Olympic* was converted at Belfast to carry some 6,000 troops, and when she was released from her war service in April 1919, she had steamed some 184,000 miles and consumed some 347,000 tons of coal. Her main engines had performed without defect and she had

The *Olympic* in dazzle paint during the First World War. Here she appears to be getting underway, an absence of smoke from her funnels. (Crown Copyright)

earned the title 'Old Reliable' and as such emerged from the shadow of the *Titanic*. A lot of this performance and reliability was surely due in part to her engine room staff and Black Gang. But following the First World War times and trends in marine engineering were changing.

In the years after the First World War, shipping companies in competition on the Atlantic withdrew their large 'express' ships one at a time for conversion to oil. The liquid fuel adopted for steam raising in boilers was petroleum, either in its crude state or more often after it had gone through a refining process, giving a treacly (viscous) black tar known as 'Bunker C oil'. The hydrogen content of oil fuel, being about 11 per cent, was higher than that of coal, which gave it an added advantage. The value of fuel oil as a heat producer was measured by its calorific value, i.e. the number of (imperial) heat units contained in 1lb of the fuel. For coal the figure for best Welsh steaming coal was 16,000 BTU, and for oil 18,500 BTU, so that 0.86lb oil was equivalent to 1lb of coal as a heat producer. Thus for a given steam production less oil fuel was required than coal. Oil fuel being a liquid could be stowed in places where coal could not, e.g. in the tanks formed by the double bottom of the ship and in existing coal

In the stokehold of a British merchant vessel, *c.*1914. Note the belt buckle secured at the back of the fireman's trousers nearest to the camera. (Crown Copyright IWM)

bunker spaces that had to be modified to make them oil tight. All bunker 'snap head' rivets had to be punched out and the holes countersunk for flush head rivets to make them leak-proof; a system of wash bulkheads was installed to restrict sloshing and free surface effect, and steam coil type heaters incorporated into the tanks to increase fluidity (less viscous). The bunker space required was less, due to the smaller quantity required for a given voyage, and also because less space was occupied per ton. The shipping of fuel oil and the handling of it on board were practically noiseless, and unaccompanied by any dust or mess.

On average it took eight months to convert a large ship; yet the resulting economies in manpower, speed of bunkering and maintenance more than offset the temporary loss of revenue. The labour required for supplying oil to the burners in the furnaces was reduced by about 75 per cent. In a coal-burning ship one fireman would attend to three furnaces, but with oil fuel one fireman could look after twelve furnaces, and with much less manual effort! In a large passenger ship as many as 200 men could be redundant in the engineering department; for those men who had once performed the back-breaking task of keeping up steam to maintain the schedules, this was their reward: to be consigned to history. For those firemen who survived the conversions and were taken on to oil-burning ships, they would acquire a white-overalled respectability that their blackened predecessors had never attained.

(It is for consideration that in the early 1920s when coal-burning gave way to oil-fired boilers that Kilroy's apparatus was made redundant and that firemen may have joked about the conditions on the coal burners with the comments like 'Kilroy was here'.)

The combustion of oil, was continuous and uniform, with a corresponding uniform production of steam and no residue, unlike with coal in which ash was continually formed in the furnaces which had to be removed and the firebed remade. All this had a bad effect on the boiler and the quantity of steam raised. Anything from 3 per cent to 20 per cent of the weight of coal could be left in the furnaces as ash. Oil-fired boilers could be more effectively controlled by shutting off the burners, so eventually, gone would be the distinctive, sulphurous reek of coal smoke around the ports, and the clouds of filth and coal dust when bunkering by coal chutes.

Another advantage of oil-firing was that smoke could be eliminated if careful control was exercised over the temperature of the oil and the air supply during combustion. No longer could the position of a large passenger ship be given away by the tell-tale voluminous clouds of black smoke which could appear on the horizon long before its silhouette was visible to an enemy U-boat.

On 12 August 1919, the *Olympic*, the survivor of its class, entered the Thompson Drydock at Belfast for the major task of converting her boilers from coal-fired to oil-fired. Her bunkers were made 'oil tight' and lined with steam pipes for heating the fuel oil to make it more fluid for pumping. Pumps and piping would convey the oil from the bunkers via filters to boiler burners and valves. Gone was the back-breaking task of shovelling coal; instead, there was a hand-controlled valve on a burner spray. When the task was completed on 25 June 1920, firemen and trimmers now had to 'jump through hoops' to qualify as firemen. There were to be thirty-three boiler room attendants, twelve cleaners and nine greasers; a total of fifty-four compared with a total of 280 that were required when she burned coal. As such the *Olympic's* engine room staff was drastically cut by

Another view in the stokehold of a British merchant vessel during the First World War. To the right in the foreground a trimmer emerges from the bunker access with a barrow load of coal. (Claes–Göran Wetterholm Archive)

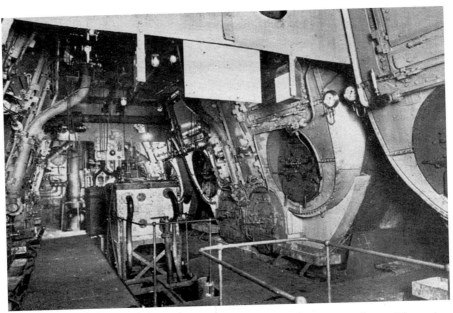

The *Aquitania*'s stokehold under oil-fired installation. She was converted to burn oil between 1919 and 1920 at a cost of £400,000. (Author's collection)

226; an ensuing saving in labour costs that was not welcomed in shipping pool circles. The accommodation space vacated by the axed personnel was rearranged for third-class passengers.

Likewise, when White Star's reparation liner, the *Homeric* (ex-*Columbus*), was converted to oil-firing from October 1923 to April 1924, her speed was only marginally increased but it had a devastating effect upon the number of her engine room staff. Apparently exact figures were never published, probably because of the bad publicity that would have been generated following growing unemployment in the UK at the time. It was estimated that the engine room staff were reduced by two-thirds to under 100.

Things were no better with rival Cunard's *Aquitania* that was converted to oil-firing from 1919–20 at a cost of £400,000, with her boiler and engine room crew reduced from 350 to 50; and their *Mauretania* of 1907 during its conversion to an oil burner in 1921, the engine room staff was reduced from 446 to 175.

Returning to the *Olympic*, as a coal-burning steamer on the North Atlantic service, average results showed: speed 21.89 knots; displacement 48,405 tons; coal burned per twenty-four hours, all purposes, 726 tons; fuel co-efficient 19,200. Later, when burning fuel oil, average figures were: speed 21.97 knots; displacement 49,890 tons; fuel oil burned per twenty-four hours, all purposes, 548 tons; fuel co-efficient 26,205.

The outlook of employment for firemen and trimmers looked bleak but White Star still had many coal-fired ships in its fleet. The 1913-built *Ceramic*, the largest triple-screw passenger ship on the Australian run, which had adopted similar combination machinery to the 'Olympic'-class, was still coal-fired. She remained so throughout her operational career with White Star until transferred to Shaw Savill & Albion following White Star's merger with Cunard in 1934. If fact, the *Ceramic* remained a coal burner up until the time she was sunk by a German U-boat in December 1942, resulting in a loss of 655 lives. In addition White Star also maintained the *Adriatic*, *Baltic*, *Cedric* and *Celtic* on the Atlantic run, and the *Athenic*, *Corinthic* and *Ionic* on the long-haul service to New Zealand; all were coal burners.

Ironically, in 1927, one of the last liners to be built for White Star was the second *Laurentic*. Her machinery bucked the trend to switch to motor propulsion, and instead her design had reverted to the earlier combination machinery of three screws with steam reciprocating units on the wing shafts, and a low-pressure turbine driving the centre propeller. She was completed as a coal burner at a time when the trend was for oil-fired boilers and her machinery system was virtually the same power plant that had

A fireman on the newly oil-fired *Aquitania* regulating the flow of oil to the furnaces. Although their tasks were less labour intensive and the environment much cleaner, they were still referred to as the Black Gang. (Author's collection)

been installed in the previous *Laurentic* of 1909! She was reputed to be the last coal-burning transatlantic liner when she entered service. Interestingly, she was taken up on 24 August 1939 and converted to an Armed Merchant Cruiser at Devonport Dockyard.

Mr J. Evans, a young marine engineer, joined the *Laurentic* for the first year of the war before he was due to take his Second Class Certificate of Competency (Second's 'ticket'). He later recalled of his time on board: 'Among the engineers were some ex-Cunarders who looked down their noses at the reciprocating engines, not to mention coal.' And of her performance on patrol and the engine room crew, he went on to add:

Even steaming at very reduced speed, about 20 days on patrol was the limit. The *Laurentic* would return to Liverpool and take on 4,000 tons of coal … We had a black gang of around 120, mostly Liverpool men. They did not take kindly to Navy discipline. On sailing day, I was relieved of my engine room duties in order to stand guard at one of the ship's side doors, complete with pistol. I was supposed to stop firemen from

On October 20, 1910, was launched the White Star liner *Olympic*, a ship which marked notable advance in ocean transport. She was over 882 feet in length, and 46,000 tons gross tonnage. Her sister ship was the *Titanic*.

Photo : Fo

The *Olympic* at Southampton in the early 1930s showing that even with oil-firing the fuel/air draught mix had to be correct. (Author's collection)

jumping ship. Some did get away, by disguising themselves as the shore gang, carrying a length of pipe on their shoulders.

A feeling of déjà vu here. Sadly, the *Laurentic* was torpedoed and sunk by a German U-boat on 4 November 1940 with a loss of forty-nine lives.

A more positive note about firemen in the Second World War is from the Imperial War Museum (document IWM 81/45/1) in which Fifth Engineer Ronald Dunshea, on board Shaw Savill & Albion's *Maimoa*, a 1920-built cargo liner, originally jointly owned by White Star, recalled:

… driven through the water by a great deal of hard manual labour on the part of the stokehold crowd … Each [fire]man [had] to feed his three furnaces with two tons of coal each four-hour watch, as well as slicing and raking the fires to ensure good consumption. [Quite a contrast to the *Titanic*'s coal consumption of 140 tons per watch.]

At the beginning of each watch ashpits had to be cleaned. A stokehold was a dirty and unpleasant place of work … the firemen and [coal]

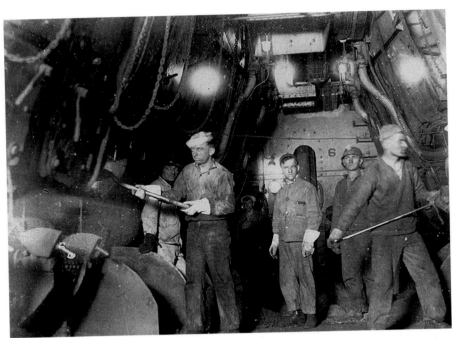

US Navy stokers on board the USS *Mount Vernon* (ex-*Kronprinzessen Cecilie*) in 1919. Here in No 4 boiler room the sailors are wearing head gear and protective gloves. The stoker on the left has his shovel upside-down which suggests he has tipped his coal rather than pitching it in. (US Naval Historical Centre)

There were still berths for firemen and trimmers on White Star's ships like the *Ceramic* on the Australian run. (Tom Rayner collection)

trimmers were a rough lot ... Each watch [was] accommodated in a single, badly ventilated room in the fo'c's'le ... At sea with a seven day week they had no diversions. In port they usually sought solace in dockland hostelries. In such establishments many seafarers fell foul of the ladies ... the effects manifesting themselves a few weeks [later].

Returning to their ship, these men, 'proclaimed in four letter words their refusal to serve England's cause'.

Yet they did, despite conditions that were appalling enough in peace time and which in war put them in a submerged 'front-line' that, being out of sight, has been put out of mind. In the event of their ship taking a torpedo amidships it was those in the boiler and engine rooms who were most likely to perish. Moreover, if they escaped drowning, being burned by hot coals or oil fuel or scalded by steam, they were likely to arrive on deck in the cold darkness of an Atlantic night dressed only in the singlet and trousers suitable to their usual place of work. In fact, in much the same way as their predecessors had done the night the *Titanic* sank back in 1912. The *Maimoa* itself was sunk by the German surface raider *Pinguin* on 20 November 1940 while in the Indian Ocean, without loss of life.

The main health hazards to the Black Gang apart from burns, scalds and falls were accumulated over time. Back problems such as lumbago, sciatica and a slipped disc could bring a premature end to one's career, or like coal miners, respiratory problems such as silicosis and pneumoconiosis.

And if a fireman or trimmer were to take a job ashore, there were openings such as boiler plants of factories and hospitals, water pumping stations, local 'electric light works' and the 'gas works'. There could be posts as firemen on locomotives in the four major railway companies that came into existence from 1 January 1923.

Coal-burning vessels carried on at sea well into the latter half of the twentieth century; in fact, Blue Funnel Line's (Alfred Holt) last coal burner, the *Diomed*, which was completed in 1922 remained in service until her disposal in September 1952!

White Star's *Laurentic* of 1927 reputed to be the last coal-burning liner on the Atlantic. (Tom Rayner collection)

The image of the fireman in the Second World War. Operating a firing rake in the gloaming of an upper furnace, his face is grim with concentration and cigarette in mouth. (Author's collection)

Chant of the Firemen (*c.*1888)

This is the steamer's pit.
The ovens like dragons of fire
Glare thro' their close-lidded eyes
With restless hungry desire.

Down from the tropic night
Rushes the funnelled air;
Our heads expand and fall in;
Our hearts thump huge as despair.

'Tis we make the bright hot blood
Of this throbbing inanimate thing;
And our life is no less the fuel
Than the coal we shovel and fling.

And lest of this we be proud
Or anything but meek,
We are all well cursed and paid–
Ten shillings a week!

Round, round, round in its tunnel
The shaft turns pitiless strong,
While lost souls cry out in the darkness:
'How long, O Lord, how long?'
(Francis Adams 1862–93)

Footnote

In the early 1960s, when the author was accepted as a marine engineer apprentice with a shipping company, upon telling his father the good news, his dad replied: 'Oh! Down Amongst the Black Gang.'

Finished with Engines

APPENDIX

LIST OF *TITANIC'S* ENGINEERING DEPARTMENT
INCLUDING ELECTRICIANS, GREASERS, FIREMEN AND TRIMMERS

Names in bold, those considered to be the Black Gang. Survivors names in italics.

Name	Age	Class/Dept	Joined	Job	Boat	Body
ABRAMS, Mr William	33	Engine	Southampton	Fireman / Stoker		
ADAMS, Mr R.	26	Engine	Southampton	Fireman / Stoker		
ALLEN, Mr Henry	32	Engine	Southampton	Fireman / Stoker		145
ALLEN, Mr Ernest Frederick	24	Engine	Southampton	Trimmer	B	
ALLSOP, Mr Alfred Samuel	34	Engine	Belfast	Electrician		
AVERY, Mr James Frank	22	Engine	Southampton	Trimmer	15	
BAILEY, Mr George W.	46	Engine	Southampton	Fireman / Stoker		
BAINES, Mr Richard	24	Engine	Southampton	Greaser		
BANNON, Mr John	32	Engine	Southampton	Greaser		
BARLOW, Mr Charles	30	Engine	Southampton	Fireman / Stoker		
BARNES, Mr Charles	29	Engine	Southampton	Fireman / Stoker		
BARNES, Mr J.	41	Engine	Southampton	Fireman / Stoker		
BARRETT, Mr Frederick	28	Engine	Southampton	Leading Fireman	13	
BARRETT, Mr Frederick William	33	Engine	Southampton	Fireman / Stoker		
BEATTIE, Mr Joseph	35	Engine	Belfast	Greaser		
BEAUCHAMP, Mr George William	24	Engine	Southampton	Fireman / Stoker	13	
BELL, Mr Joseph	50	Engine	Belfast	Chief Engineer		
BENDELL, Mr F.	24	Engine	Southampton	Fireman / Stoker		

The *Titanic*'s Engineers' Memorial at Southampton. (David L. Williams)

Name	Age	Class/Dept	Joined	Job	Boat	Body
BENNETT, Mr George Alfred	30	Engine	Southampton	Fireman / Stoker		
BENVILLE, Mr E.	42	Engine	Southampton	Fireman / Stoker		
BESSANT, Mr William Edward	39	Engine	Southampton	Fireman / Stoker		
BEVIS, Mr Joseph Henry	22	Engine	Southampton	Trimmer		
BIDDLECOMBE, Mr Charles	33	Engine	Southampton	Fireman / Stoker		
BIGGS, Mr Edward Charles	20	Engine	Southampton	Fireman / Stoker		
BILLOW, Mr J.	20	Engine	Southampton	Trimmer		
BINSTEAD, Mr Walter	19	Engine	Southampton	Trimmer	3	
BLACK, Mr Alexander	28	Engine	Southampton	Fireman / Stoker		
BLACK, Mr D.	41	Engine	Southampton	Fireman / Stoker		
BLACKMAN, Mr H.	24	Engine	Southampton	Fireman / Stoker		
BLAKE, Mr Percival Albert	22	Engine	Southampton	Trimmer		
BLAKE, Mr Seaton	26	Engine	Belfast	Mess Steward		
BLAKE, Mr Thomas	36	Engine	Southampton	Fireman / Stoker		
BLANEY, Mr James	29	Engine	Southampton	Fireman / Stoker		
BLANN, Mr Eustace Horatius	21	Engine	Southampton	Fireman / Stoker		
BOTT, Mr W.	44	Engine	Southampton	Greaser		
BRADLEY, Mr Patrick Joseph	39	Engine	Southampton	Fireman / Stoker		
BREWER, Mr Henry ('Harry')	30	Engine	Southampton	Trimmer		

Name	Age	Class/Dept	Joined	Job	Boat	Body
BRIANT, Mr Albert	34	Engine	Southampton	Greaser		
BROOKS, Mr J.	25	Engine	Southampton	Trimmer		
BROWN, Mr John	25	Engine	Southampton	Fireman / Stoker		267
BROWN, Mr Joseph James	25	Engine	Southampton	Fireman / Stoker		
BURROUGHS, Mr Arthur	35	Engine	Southampton	Fireman / Stoker		
BURTON, Mr Edward John	32	Engine	Southampton	Fireman / Stoker		
BUTT, Mr William John	30	Engine	Southampton	Fireman / Stoker		77
CALDERWOOD, Mr Hugh	30	Engine	Belfast	Trimmer		
CANNER, Mr J.	40	Engine	Southampton	Fireman / Stoker		
CARR, Mr Richard Stephen	37	Engine	Southampton	Trimmer		
CARTER (BALL), Mr James (W.)	46	Engine	Southampton	Fireman / Stoker		
CASEY, Mr T.	28	Engine	Southampton	Trimmer		
CASTLEMAN, Mr Edward	37	Engine	Southampton	Greaser		
CAVELL, Mr George Henry	22	Engine	Southampton	Trimmer		
CHERRETT, Mr William Victor	24	Engine	Southampton	Fireman / Stoker		
CHISNALL, Mr George Alexander	35	Engine	Belfast	Boilermaker		111
CHORLEY, Mr John	25	Engine	Southampton	Fireman / Stoker		
CLARK, Mr William	39	Engine	Southampton	Fireman / Stoker		
COE, Mr Harry	21	Engine	Southampton	Trimmer		
COLEMAN, Mr John	57	Engine	Belfast	Mess Steward		
COLLINS, Mr Samuel	35	Engine	Southampton	Fireman / Stoker	1	
COMBES, Mr George	34	Engine	Southampton	Fireman / Stoker		
COOPER, Mr Harry	26	Engine	Southampton	Fireman / Stoker		
COOPER, Mr James	25	Engine	Southampton	Trimmer		
COPPERTHWAITE, Mr B.	22	Engine	Southampton	Fireman / Stoker		
CORCORAN, Mr Denny	33	Engine	Southampton	Fireman / Stoker		
COTTON, Mr A.		Engine	Southampton	Trimmer		
COUCH, Mr Joseph Henry	45	Engine	Southampton	Greaser		
COUPER, Mr Robert	30	Engine	Southampton	Fireman / Stoker		
COY, Mr Francis Ernest George	26	Engine	Belfast	Junior Assistant Third Engineer		
CRABB, Mr H.	23	Engine	Southampton	Trimmer		
CREESE, Mr Henry Philip	44	Engine	Belfast	Deck Engineer		
CRIMMINS, Mr James	21	Engine	Southampton	Fireman / Stoker	13	
CROSS, Mr W.	39	Engine	Southampton	Fireman / Stoker		
CUNNINGHAM, Mr B.	30	Engine	Southampton	Fireman / Stoker		
CURTIS, Mr Arthur	25	Engine	Southampton	Fireman / Stoker		
DAVIES, Mr Thomas	33	Engine	Southampton	Leading Fireman		

Name	Age	Class/Dept	Joined	Job	Boat	Body
DAWSON, Mr Joseph	23	Engine	Southampton	Trimmer		227
DIAPER, Mr J.	24	Engine	Southampton	Fireman / Stoker		
DICKSON, Mr W.	36	Engine	Southampton	Trimmer		
DILLEY, Mr John	30	Engine	Southampton	Fireman / Stoker		
DILLON, Mr Thomas Patrick	24	Engine	Southampton	Trimmer		
DODD, Mr Edward Charles	38	Engine	Belfast	Junior Third Engineer		
DODDS, Mr Henry Watson	27	Engine	Southampton	Junior Assistant Fourth Engineer		
DOEL, Mr Frederick	22	Engine	Southampton	Fireman / Stoker		
DORE, Mr A.	22	Engine	Southampton	Trimmer		
DOYLE, Mr Laurence	27	Engine	Southampton	Fireman / Stoker		
DUFFY, Mr William Luke	28	Engine	Belfast	Writer / Engineer's Clerk		
DYER, Mr Henry Ryland	24	Engine	Belfast	Senior Assistant Fourth Engineer		
DYMOND, Mr Frank	25	Engine	Southampton	Fireman / Stoker		
EAGLE, Mr A.J.	22	Engine	Southampton	Trimmer		
EASTMAN, Mr Charles	44	Engine	Southampton	Greaser		
ELLIOTT, Mr Everett Edward	24	Engine	Southampton	Trimmer		317
ERVINE, Mr Albert George	18	Engine	Belfast	Electrician		
EVANS, Mr William	30	Engine	Southampton	Trimmer		31
FARQUHARSON, Mr William Edward	39	Engine	Belfast	Senior Second Engineer		
FAY, Mr Thomas Joseph	30	Engine	Southampton	Greaser		
FERRARY, Mr Antonio	34	Engine	Southampton	Trimmer		
FERRIS, Mr W.	38	Engine	Southampton	Leading Fireman		
FITZPATRICK, Mr Hugh J.	27	Engine	Belfast	Junior Boilermaker		
FITZPATRICK, Mr Cecil William	21	Engine	Southampton	Mess Steward		
FLARTY, Mr Edward	43	Engine	Southampton	Fireman / Stoker		
FORD, Mr H.	22	Engine	Southampton	Trimmer		
FORD, Mr Thomas	30	Engine	Southampton	Leading Fireman		
FOSTER, Mr Albert C.	37	Engine	Belfast	Storekeeper		
FRASER, Mr James	29	Engine	Belfast	Junior Assistant Third Engineer		
FRASER, Mr J.	30	Engine	Southampton	Fireman / Stoker		
FREDERICKS, Mr Walter Francis	20	Engine	Southampton	Trimmer		
FRYER, Mr Albert Ernest	26	Engine	Southampton	Trimmer		
GEER, Mr Alfred Ernest	24	Engine	Southampton	Fireman / Stoker		

Name	Age	Class/Dept	Joined	Job	Boat	Body
GODLEY, Mr George	34	Engine	Southampton	Fireman / Stoker		
GODWIN, Mr Frederick Walter	34	Engine	Southampton	Greaser		
GOLDER, Mr M.W.	32	Engine	Southampton	Fireman / Stoker		
GORDON, Mr J.	29	Engine	Southampton	Trimmer		
GOREE, Mr Frank	42	Engine	Southampton	Greaser		222
GOSLING, Mr Bertram James	22	Engine	Southampton	Trimmer		
GOSLING, Mr S.	26	Engine	Southampton	Trimmer		
GRADIDGE, Mr Ernest Edward	22	Engine	Southampton	Fireman / Stoker		276
GRAHAM, Mr Thomas G.	28	Engine	Belfast	Fireman / Stoker		
GREEN, Mr George	20	Engine	Southampton	Trimmer		
GREGORY, Mr David	40	Engine	Southampton	Greaser		
GUMERY, Mr George	24	Engine	Southampton	Mess Steward		
HAGGAN, Mr John	35	Engine	Belfast	Fireman / Stoker	3	
HALL, Mr J.	32	Engine	Southampton	Fireman / Stoker		
HALLETT, Mr George	22	Engine	Southampton	Fireman / Stoker		
HANDS, Mr Bernard	53	Engine	Southampton	Fireman / Stoker		
HANNAM, Mr George	30	Engine	Southampton	Fireman / Stoker		
HARRIS, Mr Amos Fred	21	Engine	Southampton	Trimmer		
HARRIS, Mr Edward	28	Engine	Southampton	Fireman / Stoker		
HARRIS, Mr Frederick	39	Engine	Southampton	Fireman / Stoker		
HARRISON, Mr Norman E.	38	Engine	Belfast	Junior Second Engineer		
HART, Mr James	49	Engine	Southampton	Fireman / Stoker		
HARVEY, Mr Herbert Gifford	34	Engine	Belfast	Junior Assistant Second Engineer		
HASLIN, Mr James	45	Engine	Southampton	Trimmer		
HEAD, Mr A.	24	Engine	Southampton	Fireman / Stoker		
HEBB, Mr A.	20	Engine	Southampton	Trimmer		
HENDRICKSON, Mr Charles George	29	Engine	Southampton	Leading Fireman	1	
HESKETH, Mr John Henry	33	Engine	Belfast	Engineer		
HILL, Mr James	25	Engine	Southampton	Trimmer		
HINTON, Mr Stephen William	30	Engine	Southampton	Trimmer		85
HODGE, Mr Charles	29	Engine	Belfast	Senior Assistant Third Engineer		
HODGES, Mr W.	26	Engine	Southampton	Fireman / Stoker		
HODGKINSON, Mr Leonard	46	Engine	Belfast	Senior Fourth Engineer		
HOPGOOD, Mr Roland	22	Engine	Southampton	Fireman / Stoker		
HOSGOOD, Mr Richard	22	Engine	Southampton	Fireman / Stoker		242

Name	Age	Class/Dept	Joined	Job	Boat	Body
HOSKING, Mr George Fox	36	Engine	Belfast	Senior Third Engineer		
HUNT, Mr Albert	22	Engine	Southampton	Trimmer		
HUNT, Mr Tom	28	Engine	Southampton	Fireman / Stoker		
HURST, Mr Charles John	35	Engine	Southampton	Fireman / Stoker		
HURST, Mr Walter	23	Engine	Southampton	Fireman / Stoker		
INGRAM, Mr Charles	20	Engine	Southampton	Trimmer		204
INSTANCE, Mr T.	33	Engine	Southampton	Fireman / Stoker		
JACOBSON, Mr John	29	Engine	Southampton	Fireman / Stoker		
JAGO, Mr Joseph	27	Engine	Southampton	Greaser		
JAMES, Mr Thomas	27	Engine	Southampton	Fireman / Stoker		
JARVIS, Mr Walter	37	Engine	Southampton	Fireman / Stoker		
JOAS, Mr N.	38	Engine	Southampton	Fireman / Stoker		
JUDD, Mr Charles E.	32	Engine	Southampton	Fireman / Stoker		
JUKES, Mr James	35	Engine	Southampton	Greaser		
JUPE, Mr Boykett Herbert	30	Engine	Southampton	Electrician		73
KASPER, Mr F.	40	Engine	Southampton	Fireman / Stoker		
KEARL, Mr Charles Henry	43	Engine	Southampton	Greaser		
KEARL, Mr G.	24	Engine	Southampton	Trimmer		
KEEGAN, Mr James	38	Engine	Southampton	Leading Fireman		
KELLY, Mr James	44	Engine	Southampton	Greaser		
KELLY, Mr William	23	Engine	Belfast	Assistant Electrician		
KEMISH, Mr George	24	Engine	Southampton	Fireman / Stoker		
KEMP, Mr Thomas Hulman	43	Engine	Belfast	Extra Assistant Fourth Engineer (Refrigeration)		
KENCHENTEN, Mr Frederick	37	Engine	Southampton	Greaser		
KENZLER, Mr Augustus	43	Engine	Belfast	Storekeeper		
KERR, Mr Thomas	26	Engine	Southampton	Fireman / Stoker		
KINSELLA, Mr L.	30	Engine	Southampton	Fireman / Stoker		
KIRKHAM, Mr J.	39	Engine	Southampton	Greaser		
KNOWLES, Mr Thomas	42	Engine	Southampton	Fireman Messman		
LAHY, Mr T.E.	32	Engine	Southampton	Fireman / Stoker		
LEE, Mr H.	18	Engine	Southampton	Trimmer		
LIGHT, Mr Christopher William	20	Engine	Southampton	Fireman / Stoker		
LIGHT, Mr W.	47	Engine	Southampton	Fireman / Stoker		
LINDSAY, Mr William Charles	30	Engine	Southampton	Fireman / Stoker	3	
LLOYD, Mr W.	29	Engine	Southampton	Fireman / Stoker		
LONG, Mr F.	28	Engine	Southampton	Trimmer		
LONG, Mr W.	30	Engine	Southampton	Trimmer		

Name	Age	Class/Dept	Joined	Job	Boat	Body
MACKIE, Mr William Dickson	32	Engine	Belfast	Junior Fifth Engineer		
MAJOR, Mr William James	32	Engine	Southampton	Fireman / Stoker	13	
MARRETT, Mr G.	22	Engine	Southampton	Fireman / Stoker		
MARSH, Mr Frederick Charles	39	Engine	Southampton	Fireman / Stoker		268
MASKELL, Mr Leopold Adolphus	25	Engine	Southampton	Trimmer		
MASON, Mr Frank Archibald Robert	32	Engine	Southampton	Fireman / Stoker		
MASON, Mr J.	39	Engine	Southampton	Leading Fireman		
MAY, Mr Arthur	24	Engine	Southampton	Fireman / Stoker		
MAY, Mr Arthur William	60	Engine	Southampton	Fireman Messman		
MAYO, Mr William Peter	27	Engine	Southampton	Leading Fireman		177
MAYZES, Mr Thomas	25	Engine	Southampton	Fireman / Stoker		
MCANDREW, Mr Thomas	36	Engine	Southampton	Fireman / Stoker		
MCANDREWS, Mr William	23	Engine	Southampton	Fireman / Stoker		
MCCASTLAN, Mr W.	38	Engine	Southampton	Fireman / Stoker		
MCGANN, Mr James	26	Engine	Southampton	Trimmer		
MCGARVEY, Mr Edward Joseph	34	Engine	Southampton	Fireman / Stoker		
MCGAW, Mr Eroll V.	30	Engine	Southampton	Fireman / Stoker		
MCGREGOR, Mr J.	30	Engine	Southampton	Fireman / Stoker		
MCINERNEY, Mr Thomas	37	Engine	Southampton	Greaser		
MCINTYRE, Mr William	21	Engine	Southampton	Trimmer		
MCQUILLAN, Mr William	26	Engine	Belfast	Fireman / Stoker		183
MCRAE, Mr William Alexander	32	Engine	Southampton	Fireman / Stoker		
MCREYNOLDS, Mr William	22	Engine	Belfast	Junior Sixth Engineer		
MIDDLETON, Mr Alfred Pirrie	26	Engine	Belfast	Electrician		
MILFORD, Mr George	28	Engine	Southampton	Fireman / Stoker		
MILLAR, Mr Robert	26	Engine	Belfast	Extra Fifth Engineer		
MILLAR, Mr Thomas	33	Engine	Belfast	Deck Enginer		
MINTRAM, Mr William	46	Engine	Southampton	Fireman / Stoker		
MITCHELL, Mr Lawrence	18	Engine	Southampton	Trimmer		
MOORE, Mr John J.	29	Engine	Southampton	Fireman / Stoker		
MOORE, Mr Ralph William	21	Engine	Southampton	Trimmer		
MOORES, Mr Richard Henry	44	Engine	Southampton	Greaser		
MORELL, Mr R.	21	Engine	Southampton	Trimmer		
MORGAN, Mr Arthur Herbert	27	Engine	Southampton	Trimmer		
MORGAN, Mr Thomas A.	26	Engine	Southampton	Fireman / Stoker		302
MORRIS, Mr Arthur	30	Engine	Southampton	Greaser		

Name	Age	Class/Dept	Joined	Job	Boat	Body
MORRIS, Mr W.	24	Engine	Southampton	Trimmer		
MOYES, Mr William Young	23	Engine	Belfast	Senior Sixth Engineer		
MURDOCH, Mr William John	33	Engine	Southampton	Fireman / Stoker		
NETTLETON, Mr George	28	Engine	Southampton	Fireman / Stoker		
NEWMAN, Mr Charles Thomas	33	Engine	Southampton	Assistant Storekeeper		
NOON, Mr John	35	Engine	Southampton	Fireman / Stoker		
NORRIS, Mr J.	23	Engine	Southampton	Fireman / Stoker		
NOSS, Mr Bertram Arthur	21	Engine	Southampton	Fireman / Stoker		
NOSS, Mr Henry	30	Engine	Southampton	Fireman / Stoker		
NUTBEAN, Mr William	30	Engine	Southampton	Fireman / Stoker		
O'CONNOR, Mr John	25	Engine	Southampton	Trimmer		
OLIVE, Mr Charles	31	Engine	Southampton	Greaser		
OLIVER, Mr Harry	32	Engine	Southampton	Fireman / Stoker		
OTHEN, Mr Charles	35	Engine	Southampton	Fireman / Stoker		
PAICE, Mr Richard Charles John	32	Engine	Southampton	Fireman / Stoker		
PAINTER, Mr Charles	31	Engine	Southampton	Fireman / Stoker		
PAINTER, Mr Frank Frederick	29	Engine	Southampton	Fireman / Stoker		
PALLES, Mr Thomas	42	Engine	Belfast	Greaser		
PARSONS, Mr Frank Alfred	26	Engine	Belfast	Senior Fifth Engineer		
PEARCE, Mr John	28	Engine	Southampton	Fireman / Stoker		
PELHAM, Mr George	39	Engine	Southampton	Trimmer	16	
PERRY, Mr Edgar Lionel	19	Engine	Southampton	Trimmer		
PERRY, Mr H.	23	Engine	Southampton	Trimmer		
PHILLIPS, Mr A.G.	27	Engine	Southampton	Greaser		
PITFIELD, Mr William James	25	Engine	Southampton	Greaser		
PODESTA, Mr John Alexander	24	Engine	Southampton	Fireman / Stoker		
POND, Mr George	32	Engine	Southampton	Fireman / Stoker		
PRANGNELL, Mr George Alexander	30	Engine	Southampton	Greaser		
PRESTON, Mr Thomas Charles Alfred	20	Engine	Southampton	Trimmer		
PRIEST, Mr Arthur John	24	Engine	Southampton	Fireman / Stoker		
PROUDFOOT, Mr Richard	23	Engine	Southampton	Trimmer		
PUGH, Mr Percy	31	Engine	Southampton	Leading Fireman		
PUSEY, Mr Robert William	24	Engine	Southampton	Fireman / Stoker	1	
RANGER, Mr Thomas	29	Engine	Southampton	Greaser	4	

Name	Age	Class/Dept	Joined	Job	Boat	Body
READ, Mr J.	21	Engine	Southampton	Trimmer		
READ, Mr Robert	30	Engine	Southampton	Trimmer		
REEVES, Mr F.	31	Engine	Southampton	Fireman / Stoker		180
RICE, Mr Charles	32	Engine	Southampton	Fireman / Stoker		
RICHARDS, Mr Joseph James	28	Engine	Southampton	Fireman / Stoker		
RICKMAN, Mr George Albert	36	Engine	Southampton	Fireman / Stoker		
ROBERTS, Mr Robert George	35	Engine	Southampton	Fireman / Stoker		
ROUS, Mr Arthur J.	26	Engine	Belfast	Plumber		
RUDD, Mr Henry	23	Engine	Southampton	Assistant Storekeeper		86
RUTTER (GRAVES), Mr Sidney Frank	30	Engine	Southampton	Fireman / Stoker		
SANGSTER, Mr Charles	32	Engine	Southampton	Fireman / Stoker		
SAUNDERS, Mr F.	23	Engine	Southampton	Fireman / Stoker		
SAUNDERS, Mr Walter Edward	23	Engine	Southampton	Trimmer		0
SAUNDERS, Mr W.	23	Engine	Southampton	Fireman / Stoker		184
SCOTT, Mr Frederick William	28	Engine	Southampton	Greaser		
SCOTT, Mr Archibald	40	Engine	Southampton	Fireman / Stoker		
SELF, Mr Alfred Henry	39	Engine	Southampton	Greaser		
SELF, Mr Edward	25	Engine	Southampton	Fireman / Stoker		
SENIOR, Mr Harry	31	Engine	Southampton	Fireman / Stoker		
SHEA, Mr Thomas	32	Engine	Southampton	Fireman / Stoker		
SHEATH, Mr Frederick	20	Engine	Southampton	Trimmer	1	
SHEPHERD, Mr Jonathan	32	Engine	Southampton	Junior Assistant Second Engineer		
SHIERS, Mr Alfred Charles	25	Engine	Southampton	Fireman / Stoker		
SHILLABEER, Mr Charles Frederick	20	Engine	Southampton	Trimmer		195
SKEATES, Mr William	26	Engine	Southampton	Trimmer		
SLOAN, Mr Peter	31	Engine	Belfast	Chief Electrician		
SMALL, Mr William	40	Engine	Southampton	Leading Fireman		
SMITH, Mr Emest George	26	Engine	Southampton	Trimmer		
SMITH, Mr James M.	35	Engine	Belfast	Junior Fourth Engineer		
SMITHER, Mr Harry John	22	Engine	Southampton	Fireman / Stoker		
SNELLGROVE, Mr G.	40	Engine	Southampton	Fireman / Stoker		
SNOOKS, Mr W.	26	Engine	Southampton	Trimmer		
SNOW, Mr Eustace Philip	21	Engine	Southampton	Trimmer		
SPARKMAN, Mr H.	30	Engine	Southampton	Fireman / Stoker		

Name	Age	Class/Dept	Joined	Job	Boat	Body
STANBROOK, Mr Alfred Augustus	30	Engine	Southampton	Fireman / Stoker		316
STEEL, Mr Robert Edward		Engine	Southampton	Trimmer		
STOCKER, Mr H.	20	Engine	Southampton	Trimmer		
STREET, Mr Thomas Albert	25	Engine	Southampton	Fireman/Stoker		
STUBBS, Mr James Henry	28	Engine	Southampton	Fireman/Stoker		
SULLIVAN, Mr S.	25	Engine	Southampton	Fireman / Stoker		
TAYLOR, Mr J.	42	Engine	Southampton	Fireman / Stoker		
TAYLOR, Mr James	24	Engine	Southampton	Fireman / Stoker	1	
TAYLOR, Mr John	50	Engine	Southampton	Fireman / Stoker		
TAYLOR, Mr William Henry	26	Engine	Southampton	Fireman / Stoker		
THOMAS, Mr Joseph	25	Engine	Southampton	Fireman / Stoker		
THOMPSON, Mr John William	35	Engine	Southampton	Fireman / Stoker	A	
THRELFALL, Mr Thomas	44	Engine	Southampton	Leading Fireman		
THRESHER, Mr George Terrill	25	Engine	Southampton	Fireman / Stoker	9	
TIZARD, Mr Arthur	31	Engine	Southampton	Fireman / Stoker		
TOZER, Mr James	30	Engine	Southampton	Greaser		
TRIGGS, Mr Robert	40	Engine	Southampton	Fireman / Stoker		
TURLEY, Mr Richard	35	Engine	Belfast	Fireman / Stoker		
VAN DER BRUGGE, Mr Wessel Adrianus	42	Engine	Southampton	Fireman / Stoker		
VEAL, Mr Arthur	35	Engine	Southampton	Greaser		
VEAR, Mr H.	32	Engine	Southampton	Fireman / Stoker		
VEAR, Mr William	33	Engine	Southampton	Fireman / Stoker		59
WARD, Mr Arthur	24	Engine	Belfast	Junior Assistant Fourth Engineer		
WARD, Mr J.	31	Engine	Southampton	Leading Fireman		
WARDNER, Mr Albert	39	Engine	Southampton	Fireman / Stoker		
WATERIDGE, Mr Edward Lewis	25	Engine	Southampton	Fireman / Stoker		
WATSON, Mr W.	27	Engine	Southampton	Fireman / Stoker		158
WATTS, Mr	36	Engine	Southampton	Trimmer		
WEBB, Mr S.	28	Engine	Southampton	Trimmer		
WEBBER, Mr Francis Albert	31	Engine	Southampton	Leading Fireman		
WHITE, Mr Alfred	32	Engine	Southampton	Greaser		
WHITE, Mr Frank Leonard	28	Engine	Southampton	Trimmer		
WHITE, Mr William George	23	Engine	Southampton	Trimmer		
WILLIAMS, Mr Samuel S.	26	Engine	Southampton	Fireman / Stoker		
WILSON, Mr Bertie	28	Engine	Belfast	Senior Assistant Second Engineer		

Name	Age	Class/Dept	Joined	Job	Boat	Body
WILTON, Mr William	45	Engine	Southampton	Trimmer		
WITCHER, Mr Albert Ernest	39	Engine	Southampton	Fireman / Stoker		
WITT, Mr Henry Dennis	37	Engine	Southampton	Fireman / Stoker		
WOOD, Mr Henry	30	Engine	Southampton	Trimmer		
WOODFORD, Mr Frederick	40	Engine	Southampton	Greaser		163
WYETH, Mr James	26	Engine	Southampton	Fireman / Stoker		
YOUNG, Mr Francis James	30	Engine	Southampton	Fireman / Stoker		

References re Crew Particulars of Engagement (other lists on Encyclopaedia Titanica): *Agreement and Account of Crew* (PRO London, BT100/259) PRO, London Reference BT 100/259 (handwritten piece of paper, lined), *Particulars of Engagement* (Belfast), Ulster Folk and Transport Museum (TRANS 2A/45 381)

Contributors: Hermann Söldner, Germany; Brian Ticehurst, UK

Stokers feeding the furnaces on a British battleship during the First World War. (Crown Copyright IWM)

BIBLIOGRAPHY

Admiralty, Naval Marine Engineering Practice Vol I- BR 3003(1) (HMSO, 1959).

Barratt, Nick, *Lost Voices from the* Titanic (Preface Publishing, 2009).

Bates, Lt Cdr L.M., *The Merchant Service* (Frederick Muller Ltd).

Beesley, Lawrence, *The Loss of the SS* Titanic (William Heineman, 1912).

Bristow, D.E., Titanic-*Sinking the Myths* (Katco Literary, 1995).

Daish, Herbert, John Forrest, Joseph Sword & William Embleton, *Reed's Engineering for Masters, Mates and Junior Engineers* (Thomas Reed & Co. Ltd N/D).

de Kerbrech, Richard, *Ships of the White Star Line* (Ian Allan, 2009).

Douglas, Gavin, *Seamanship for Passengers* (John Lehmann Ltd, 1949).

Duncan, J., *Steam and Other Engines* (Macmillan & Co. Ltd, 1907 & 1950).

Fisher, W.A., *Engineering for Nautical Students* (Brown, Son & Ferguson Ltd, 1936).

Gordon, W.J, *The Way of the World at Sea* (The Religious Tract Society, 1896).

Haynes, RMS Titanic *Owners' Workshop Manual* (Haynes Publishing, 2011).

Horsnaill, W.O., *Understanding Marine Engines by Q & A* (English Universities Press, 1943).

Hutchings, David F., *The* Titanic *Story* (The History Press, 2008).

Lightoller, Commander Charles E., Titanic *and Other Ships* (Bay Tree Books, N/D).

Liversidge, John G., *Engine Room Practice – A Handbook for the Royal Navy & Mercantile Marine* (Charles Griffin & Co., 1911).

McCaughan, Michael, *Steel Ships & Iron Men* (Friar's Bush Press, 1989).

MacGibbon, W.C., Arch Martin & Hugh Barr, *B.o.T. Orals and Marine Engineering Knowledge, 6th edn* (James Munro & Co. Ltd, N/D).

Mason, Michael, Greenhill, Basil & Craig, Robin, *The British Seafarer* (Hutchinson/BBC, 1980).

Maxtone-Graham, John, *The North Atlantic Run* (Cassell & Co. Ltd, 1972).

Milton, J.H., *Marine Steam Boilers* (George Newnes Ltd, 1961).

Ramsay, R.J., *Paddle Steamer Machinery – A Layman's Guide* (PSPS, 2000).

Ripper, William, *Heat Engines* (Longmans, Green & Co.).

Sennett, R. & H.J. Oram, *The Marine Steam Engine* (Longmans & Co., 1898).

Shipbuilder, *The Ocean Liners of the Past*: Olympic & Titanic (Patrick Stephens, 1976).

Sothern, J.M.W., *'Verbal' Notes and Sketches for Marine Engineer Officers, 11th edn* (Crosby, Lockwood & Son, 1924).

Thomas Andrews Notebook (Lagan Boat Company, 2009).

Tod & McGibbon, *B.o.T. Question and Answers for Marine Engineers* (James Munro & Co. Ltd, 1917 and 1918).

Todd, John A., *The Shipping World* (Sir Isaac Pitman & Sons, Ltd, 1929).

Articles, Lecture Notes and Technical Papers

Braunschweiger, Art, Titanic's Engine Rooms – Parts 1&2 (Titanic Research & Modelling Association, February 2006, March 2006).

Braunschweiger, Art, *Feeding the Fires – Boilers, Firemen & Trimmers* (Titanic Research & Modelling Association, August 2005).

Georgiou, Ioannis, *Titanic Collision and Sinking Mysteries – Part 2* (British Titanic Society-ADB, September 2009).

Griffiths, Dr Denis, *The Engineers Lost Aboard* Titanic (Web).

South Shields Marine & Technical College, *Correspondence Course for Marine Engineer Cadets* (1963–65).

Marriot, Edward, *When Ships Burned Coal* (Sea Breezes, April 1974).

Passing of an Era – The Use of Coal in Blue Funnel Ships 1866–1952 (Rhiw/Web)

Pounder, C.C., *Human Problems in Marine Engineering* (Transactions, The Institute of Marine Engineers, 1960).

Halpern, Samuel, *Titanic's Prime Mover – An Examination of Propulsion and Power* (Encyclopedia-Titanica, 2007).

TRMA, *Coal Ports and Coaling Outriggers* (TRMA, September 2005).

TRMA, *Coal Bunker Fire* (TRMA n/d).

www.encyclopedia-titanica.org
www.maritimequest.com
www.titanic-model.com
www.titanic-titanic.com

INDEX

If you enjoyed this book, you may also be interested in…

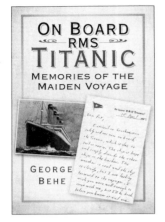

On Board RMS Titanic
GEORGE BEHE

For the first time, in this moving new book, *Titanic's* passengers and crewmen are permitted to tell the story of that lamentable disaster entirely in their own words. Included are letters, postcards, diary entries and memoirs that were written before, during and immediately after the maiden voyage itself. Many of the pre-sailing documents were composed by people who later lost their lives in the sinking and represent the last communications that these people ever had with their friends and loved ones at home.

978 0 7524 8306 1

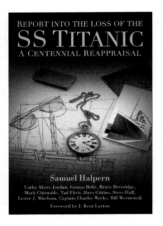

Report into the Loss of the SS Titanic
SAMUEL HALPERN ET AL.

Samuel Halpern has written many books and articles on *Titanic* and often used the 1912 wreck report as a source of reference. But what, with the knowledge we have today, would a modern-day report look like? In this book we have the answer. Sam has gathered a team of experts to write the ultimate *Titanic* reference book. Following the basic layout of the report, this team provides fascinating insights into the ship herself, the inquiries, the passengers and crew, the fateful journey and ice warnings received, the damage and sinking, protocol and process of rescue, the circumstances in connection with SS *Californian* and SS *Mount Temple*, and the aftermath and ramifications around the world.

978 0 7524 6210 3

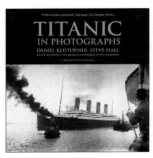

Titanic in Photographs
DANIEL KLISTORNER, STEVE HALL ET AL.

The name *Titanic* has become synonymous with catastrophe, the story of this luxurious liner legendary. In this evocative collection of photographs the authors of *Titanic The Ship Magnificent* tell her full story, from the shipyards of Harland & Wolff and its early vessels, with the backdrop of the great race to build the biggest and best passenger liner, to the frenzy of excitement surrounding her launch. Looking at her officers and crew, as well as her stops at Cherbourg and Queenstown – including some special, rare photographs – the book follows the story to its inevitable conclusion, considering the lifeboats, the presence of the *Carpathia* and the aftermath of the disaster.

978 0 7524 5896 0

Visit our website and discover thousands of other History Press books.

www.thehistorypress.co.uk